Distinctions with a Difference:

Essays on Myth, History, and Scripture in Honor of John N. Oswalt

First Fruits Press
The Academic Open Press of Asbury Theological Seminary
204 N. Lexington Ave., Wilmore, KY 40390
859-858-2236
first.fruits@asburyseminary.edu
asbury.to/firstfruits

Distinctions with a Difference: Essays on Myth, History, and Scripture in Honor of John N. Oswalt

Editors
Bill T. Arnold
&
Lawson G. Stone

Distinctions with a difference: essays on myth, history, and scripture in honor of John N. Oswalt
Editors, Bill T. Arnold & Lawson G. Stone.

First Fruits Press, ©2017

ISBN: 9781621716969 (print), 9781621716976 (digital), 9781621716983 (kindle)

Digital version at http://place.asburyseminary.edu/academicbooks/20/

First Fruits Press
B.L. Fisher Library
Asbury Theological Seminary
204 N. Lexington Ave.
Wilmore, KY 40390
http://place.asburyseminary.edu/firstfruits

Distinctions with a difference : essays on myth, history, and scripture in honor of John N. Oswalt / editors, Bill T. Arnold & Lawson G. Stone. -- Wilmore, Kentucky : First Fruits Press, ©2017.
    211 pages: illustrations ; cm.
    Festschrift for John N. Oswalt.
    Preface / Dennis F. Kinlaw -- Foreword / Timothy C. Tennent -- A singular Israel in a pluralistic world / Bill T. Arnold --A prophet like Moses? Who or why? / Daniel I. Block -- Did they know what we think they knew? Reading Genesis 2-3 iconographically / Christina Bosserman -- Paganism, Wesley and the means of grace / Joseph R. Dongell -- Isaiah's model house / Nancy L. Erickson -- A prophet unlike Moses: Balaam as prophetic intercessor / L. Daniel Hawk -- The function of Psalmic prayers in Chronicles: literary-rhetorical method in conversation with ritual theory / Michael D. Matlock -- The song of the sea and the subversion of Canaanite myth: a missional reading / Brian D. Russell – "I'm gonna make you famous" (Joshua 6:23-27) / Lawson G. Stone -- Yet another try on Job 42:6 / David L. Thompson.
    Includes bibliographical references.
    ISBN - 13: 9781621716969 (pbk.)
    1. Bible. Old Testament -- Theology. 2. Bible. Old Testament -- Criticism, interpretation, etc. 3. Oswalt, John N. 1940- I. Title. II. Arnold, Bill T. III. Stone, Lawson Grant, 1955- IV. Oswalt, John N. 1940-

BS1192.5.D57 2017   230/.0411

Cover design by Jon Ramsay

Table of Contents

Preface

As the years have passed I have found myself more conscious of the blessings that God in his graciousness has given to me in personal friendships with some very remarkable people. One of the most outstanding of these has been the one I have enjoyed with John and Karen Oswalt. I met John when he was an undergraduate at Taylor University. It was a context in which we were able to share in some intimacy our common personal faith in Christ. It established a friendship that has continued to the present day. Imagine my surprise when I found him sitting in my class in Old Testament at Asbury Theological Seminary. After he finished his work at Asbury, John began his doctoral studies at Brandeis under the great Semitic professor, Cyrus H. Gordon, under whom I had done my own doctoral studies. Then we had a very close friendship as he gave himself to the students of Asbury Theological Seminary and Wesley Biblical Seminary. Over the years our friendship deepened, and I found in it so much to enrich my personal life and my understanding of the Biblical text.

It became clear to me that John was coming to a remarkably rich understanding of the illative picture of the Messiah in the Old Testament. That meant that I was especially grateful when the editorial staff of the New International Commentary on the Old Testament decided to ask John to write the commentary on Isaiah for their commentary series. The result is his two volumes on Isaiah in which we may well have the best commentary ever written on this very important Biblical book. My suspicion is that John may know the Hebrew text of Isaiah as well as anyone in the history of biblical commentary. His understanding of the close relationship of the prophesy of Isaiah to the presentation of Christ in the New Testament gospels is intellectually and spiritually exceptional and leaves all who read him in his debt.

John has had a success in the classroom. He has been a powerful influence on a large number of students in biblical studies in his generation. Because of these students, the church of tomorrow will be able to enlarge its understanding of the message which God has given in the biblical text. We would be remiss if we did not express our gratitude to John and Karen for the fact that they have given their lives that we might understand better the eternal Word of God, especially the Old

Testament, as God's gift to us for our joy and for our salvation. The contributors to this *Festschrift* are helping us pay that debt. We thank them.

Dennis F. Kinlaw
Professor of Old Testament Languages and Literature
Asbury Theological Seminary (1963-1968)
President of Asbury College (1968-1981, 1986-1991)

Foreward

The Dominican philosopher Ralph Powell once said, "It is hard to see the whole picture when you are inside the frame." This statement underscores one of the most difficult challenges facing Christian readers of the Old Testament; namely, the hermeneutical challenge of reading the text simultaneously from two perspectives. On the one hand, every text of the Old Testament is rooted in the authentic particularity of its own cultural, historical and textual setting. Every prophecy, psalm, wisdom saying, or historical account retains its own distinctive message within all the normal cultural and linguistic parameters that defines authentic communication within specific settings. On the other hand, there is a larger frame that we must be attentive to. We must also recognize the peculiar quality of divine inspiration and revelation such that all biblical texts are framed within the larger setting of God's self-disclosure, the *missio Dei*, and the unfolding drama of redemption, which finds its climax in the person, and work of Jesus Christ.

Nowhere is this dramatic tension more readily on display than when the Apostle John brings together two quotations from Isaiah 53 and Isaiah 6 and then, quite boldly states, "Isaiah said this because he saw Jesus' glory and spoke about him" (John 12:41). Clearly Isaiah is speaking in two ways. He is speaking about the suffering of Israel, but he is also anticipating the even more profound suffering of the coming messiah. Seeing both frames is essential for good biblical interpretation. Indeed, it is the capacity to read texts from both perspectives that empowers the author of Hebrews to introduce a series of quotations from the Old Testament and yet puts them in the lips of Jesus with the remarkable statement, "Jesus is not ashamed to call them brothers. He says..." (Heb. 2:11f). Many more illustrations could be shown, all demonstrating the inspired capacity of the early church to read texts simultaneously within their own setting as well as within the larger setting of God's unfolding plan of redemption.

Few scholars have grappled with these twin realities more than the Brandeis trained professor John Oswalt, for whom these essays are dedicated. His two-volume work in Isaiah, in particular, established him as a leading scholar in Old Testament studies. His perspective on the messianic texts of Isaiah, which simultaneously honors both their original setting and their prophetic power, is arguably unparalleled among Old Testament scholars. He knows how to work within the frame of a particular text without losing sight of the larger frame of the great meta-narrative of redemption.

Dr. Oswalt has also distinguished himself as a classroom teacher. His decades of mentoring students at Wesley Biblical Seminary and Asbury Theological Seminary have brought forth a lasting legacy in the lives and ministries of his students. If it is true that our greatest work is not what we accomplish, but what we enable others to accomplish, then only heaven will fully tell the story of the impact of the life and teaching of Dr. John Oswalt. His unwavering commitment to the word of God, his rigorous scholarship and his unflinching commitment to go where the text leads him has inspired several generations of younger scholars who continue to serve within the great historic tradition of the church. The multiplying effect of mentoring is as ancient as Jesus pouring himself into his disciples, and as contemporary as the latest graduation exercise. This is the very nature of biblical discipleship.

This volume is a Festschrift honoring the scholarly legacy and teaching of John Oswalt. Each contributor in this volume has been a colleague or an associate of his, and therefore it serves as a wonderful testimony honoring his life and teaching. I commend these essays with the same simultaneous reading as Dr. Oswalt has so nobly advanced. May each essay be read within the context of its own contribution to advancing Old Testament scholarship. Yet, may each also be read within the larger context of the collective word of appreciation from the academic community for the legacy of Dr. John Oswalt as a preacher, a scholar, a mentor and one who, above all, has given his life to the extension of the glorious gospel of our Lord Jesus Christ.

Timothy C. Tennent, PhD
Professor of World Christianity
President, Asbury Theological Seminary

A Singular Israel in a Pluralistic World[1]

BILL T. ARNOLD

KEYWORDS:

Israelite worship, Temple, sacrifices, sacred festivals

Bill T. Arnold (PhD, Hebrew Union College – Jewish Institute of Religion) is the Paul S. Amos Professor of Old Testament Interpretation at Asbury Theological Seminary in Wilmore, Kentucky.

Abstract

The question of Israel's distinctiveness in the ancient Near East was a central concern of the biblical theology movement in the mid-twentieth century. The excessive claims and overstatements of that movement were corrected later in the twentieth century. Most scholars today assume the question is settled in a consensus that Old Testament Israel was not distinctive, and was completely at home in the ancient world in every respect. This paper explores three ways in which ancient Israel was indeed at home in ancient Near Eastern culture, while also suggesting ways in which Israel's religious convictions led to a genuinely unique profile in the ancient world.

INTRODUCTION

The Church has struggled throughout Christian history with precisely how the people of God are "in the world" but not "of the world" (John 17:11,14,16). The *missio Dei* has at times been complicated, or even jeopardized, by the assumptions that culture and societal norms are somehow identified with the core of Christian faith. Expression of human institutions familiar to a particular (often Western) cultural expression of Christianity can become enmeshed with the Gospel, complicating the task of cross-cultural communication of the message. The early Church, by which I mean the first three centuries of Christian antiquity that Wesley called the "primitive church," provides examples of how we can think outside our cultural boxes in preaching the Gospel, as can of course the New Testament itself (for example, illustrated by the Jerusalem Council of Acts 15; Arnold 2014:63-83).

In recent years I have come to believe that in order for the Church to overcome these stumbling blocks to adequate cross-cultural communication of the Gospel, we must go further back in our faith heritage. We need to reach deeper into our roots in ancient Israelite religion to find even better examples of cross-cultural communication of the message of God. In this brief study, I offer three examples from Israelite culture to illustrate the point. Along the way, I hope to honor Professor Oswalt's career-long focus on Israel's distinctive worldview – one of transcendence over and against continuity – which goes a long way toward explaining ancient Israel's distinctiveness (Oswalt 2009:185-94).

At the outset of this investigation, one caveat to keep in mind is that anthropologists acknowledge a certain uniformity in human experience that makes cultural comparisons tenuous. In some ways, what we experience in life today is not all that different from ancient societies, or what is sometimes called "primitive" cultures (a term not intended to be derogatory). At the same time, we must consider the variety in human experience, and focus on what Mary Douglas has called the "differences which make comparison worthwhile" (2002[1966]:96).[2] And so, I shall be considering three key cultural similarities between the Israelites and their nearest neighbors in the ancient world, while at the same time asking about the differences that make these observations compelling.

It seems perfectly obvious that no culture, ancient or modern, is created *ex nihilo* – whole cloth, or "out of nothing." And so it was with ancient Israel. The three features I will highlight here demonstrate that ancient Israel "absorbed freely from their neighbors, but not quite freely" (Douglas 2002[1966]:61). Many cultural elements of their neighbors in the ancient Near East were compatible with the worldview they inherited and continued to develop throughout their history, while others were clearly incompatible. Our objective in this exercise is to offer an interpretation of those ideological differences by highlighting the cultural similarities.

THE TEMPLE PATTERN

The familiar three-part pattern of the Solomonic temple is clear enough from textual references (1 Kgs 6:1-5), and paralleled by the structure of the tabernacle in the wilderness (e.g., Exod 26:31-37). The architectural plan of both structures, tabernacle and temple, divided and organized Israel's worship life in accord with God's boundaries established at creation between the holy and the common – the three-part pattern organizing space into ordered and graduated zones of holiness (Haran 1985:158-77). The series of enclosures draws one in by increasing degrees of holiness as one moves from the common world outside to the sacred space of the courtyard, then to the holy place, and finally to the holiest of holy places. Such an architectural design invited a direct approach to the deity in the inner sanctum, which was the last enclosed portion of the building. The graduated zones of holiness are made manifest by other features such as furniture, priestly appurtenances, and utensils used in service to YHWH.

For purposes of this investigation, we note simply that the design, structure, and to a certain extent function of this sanctuary pattern is completely at home in the Syro-Palestinian world of the southern Levant. Specifically, we have known for some time that such tripartite architectural structure was characteristic of cult sites and temples in the region among Phoenician exemplars, even stretching back to second-millennium Syrian and third-millennium Anatolian precursors (Fritz 1987:38-49).[3] I do not mean to suggest that all Levantine cult sites and worship centers had such a structure; in fact, the archaeology suggests a great diversity of patterns used.[4] On the other hand, we can trace the three-part design back through several times and places to Israel's neighbors in the Levant as one particular shared cultural feature of temples. In the most thorough study of this topic to date, Michael B. Hundley observes that among a great deal of variety in Syro-Palestinian temples of the Middle Bronze Age to the Iron Age, there are nonetheless several shared features, confirming what Amihai Mazar has called a "common" temple pattern of the time (Hundley 2013:107-18). The best attested form of this pattern includes temples with a broad porch or vestibule (often with two columns, like Jakin and Boaz; 1 Kgs 7:21; 2 Chr 3:17), a long sanctuary, and often within the sanctuary, an inner sanctuary or sanctum.

And so, we might conclude, ancient Israel was no different from its neighbors in having such a sacred space for worship. And yet, here we find the difference between Israel and the other people groups of the ancient Near East that 'makes this comparison worthwhile,' as Mary Douglas would say. This inner sanctum in other temples was constructed, without fail as far as we can determine, to house the deity in the form of a sacred statue. Such statues in Syria-Palestine represented the deity in one of four well-attested forms: anthropomorphic, theriomorphic, mixed, or as inanimate objects (Hundley 2013:342-43). Indeed, we need to widen the discussion beyond Syria-Palestine in this observation, in order to say that similar cult sites and temples throughout the ancient Near East, including Egypt, Mesopotamia, and the Anatolian Hittites, exhibited "a remarkable general commonality…regarding conceptions of deity and divine presence" (Hundley 2013:363). That remarkable commonality can be summarized as representing the major gods in cult images or statues, making communication with the deity possible, and to some degree, making control of the deity attainable. Israel's neighbors represented their gods in cult images that were typically small enough to be housed and sheltered in the confines of a temple inner sanctum. This is precisely what makes Israel's "ark of the covenant" so remarkable, as a throne representing a visible sign of the invisible presence of YHWH. One text contains what appears to have been the full name of the ark: "the ark of the covenant of YHWH of hosts, who is enthroned on the cherubim" (1 Samuel 4:4, NRSV; Arnold 2003:94-95). For Israel, YHWH was perceived as inhabiting their inner sanctum without iconic representation,[5] and that inner sanctum was perceived as a throne room for the cosmic King. Instead of a statue representing YHWH, the Israelites were distinctive in having an empty throne, in which YHWH was known to have reigned supreme over the earth. And in this also, Israel was distinctive, because no ancient Near Eastern deity was perceived as "supreme in power, presence, or perception" (Hundley 2013:363). The remarkable similarities of Israel's tabernacle/temple only highlight the differences in their perception of God.

The Sacrifices

Israel's way of speaking about animal sacrifice was another shared feature of Syro-Palestinian culture during the Late Bronze and Iron Ages. We do not have the kind of impressive evidence for sacrifice as we saw for temple architecture, owing of course to the simple fact that archaeology does not afford the physical evidence for such practices beyond structures that we typically identify as altars. For example, of the forty-five limestone altars (33 horned and 12 without horns; cf. Exod 30:1-7) excavated in the Levant, approximately half have been associated with the Israelites (Nielsen 1986:28-29). Most scholars assume, for good reason, that the Israelites incorporated Canaanite altars and priestly vessels rather than developing their own special types of altars. And yet, these are routinely difficult data to interpret, and leave us questioning at times the precise practices at work. However, we can say without equivocation that (1) Israel did indeed practice animal sacrifice, as did most peoples of the ancient world, especially throughout Mesopotamia and Syria-Palestine, and more specifically that (2) for at least a few of Israel's neighbors in the Levant, the terminology used to describe the types of sacrifices was quite similar.

The Old Testament text gives a vivid portrait of Israel's sacrificial system. Of the animal sacrifices, Israel had four basic types: the burnt offering (Lev 1), the sacrifice of well-being (Lev 3), the purgation offering (Lev 4:1–5:13), and the guilt offering (Lev 5:14–6:7).[6] In all likelihood, Canaanite sacrifices were the same, or at least, very similar to the first two Israelite offerings in this list. The origins of such animal sacrifices are clouded in mystery. It appears that the basic sacrifice of slaughter (*zebah*), what I have called here the sacrifice of well-being, was Israel's oldest expression of worship derived from pre-conquest desert traditions. This term has Ugaritic parallels (from the thirteenth century BC in the northern Levant) suggesting the meat of the slaughtered animal was eaten by the worshipper, and in Israel, perhaps only its fat was burned in sacrifice to YHWH (Milgrom 1991:218). The burnt offering (*ʿōlâ*) also seems original to Canaan and others in the Mediterranean cultures (de Vaux 1961:438-41). Unlike the *zebah*-sacrifice, this "ascending offering" (connotation of the Hebrew name) is turned completely into rising smoke and disappears before YHWH, leaving nothing to be consumed by the human worshipper. The Ugaritians had a similar concept in their "burnt sacrifice" (the noun *šrp* from the verb "to burn"), which confirms that the Israelites shared this practice with their neighbors in the Levant, some even suggesting the Israelites inherited this particular practice from the Canaanites (Kellermann 2001:98).[7]

The frequent combination of these two, "burnt offering and sacrifice," covers the category of animals offered on the altar to God. In fact, one verse suggests that Jethro, Moses' father-in-law, who was a priest of Midian, taught Moses and Aaron in the proper ways of animal sacrifice using precisely these two types of offering (Exod 18:12). And so we seem justified in seeing here another way in which Israel was completely at home in the southern Levant, sharing in practice, perception, and in at least one case, even the linguistic specifics of offerings and sacrifices. Yet it is precisely in the similarities that we once again detect profound distinctiveness in the Israelite worldview. These two basic types were also transformed by ancient Israel from the concept of feeding and appeasement of the deities into "an act of donation to, communion with, or exculpation by the deity" (Hallo 1987:6). While sacrifices in the ancient world were thought to appease the deity to ensure continued relationship, and especially to ensure continued divine favor, slaughter-sacrifices and offerings became more in Israelite thought. And this is especially manifested in Israel's development of unique additional offerings, such as the purgation offering (Lev 4:1–5:13, also called "sin offering"), and the guilt offering (Lev 5:14–6:7). The former purged or purified the inner sanctuary of Israel's temple/tabernacle, and made forgiveness for the offender possible. The guilt offering was a subcategory of the purgation offering, was also expiatory, providing forgiveness for the Israelite worshipper by focusing on reparations. So far, we have no such carefully conceived uses of sacrifice elsewhere in the ancient Near East; only Israel was so devoted to animal sacrifice as a means of purification of the temple and people, as well as forgiveness and restoration. On the contrary, animal sacrifice was used at times, especially in Mesopotamia, as a means of clairvoyance to discern future actions of the deity, especially by means of extispicy, the divinatory practice of "reading" a dead animal's entrails for signs of activity in the divine realm. Not only are all such divinatory practices related to animal sacrifice absent in ancient Israel, but in a remarkable contrast, Israel linked the entire sacrificial system to their covenantal relationship with YHWH. Canonically, the instructions for sacrifice are placed at the heart of the Torah (Lev 1-7), and historically they are placed at the foot of Mount Sinai during the last month and a half the people were encamped there (Exod 40:17; Num 10:11). Nothing comparable to this use of animal sacrifice occurs among other peoples of the ancient Near East, where such sacrifice was thought to return life or energy to its divine source, restoring the power of that source for the good of nature and humanity. Israel's view of a singular deity, YHWH, as independent and self-sustaining, meant their views and practices of animal sacrifices were distinctive.[8]

THE HOLIDAYS AND HOLY DAYS

Under this category, I have in mind Israel's festival calendars, which are detailed in five texts of the Torah: Exod 23:14-17; 34:18-26; Lev 23; Num 28-29; and Deut 16:1-17. In this brief treatment, I can only take up the role of the Sabbath (Lev 23:3) and the three pilgrimage festivals (*haggim*) of early Israel, which also receive most attention in these texts: Passover (Lev 23:4-8), the Feast of Weeks or Pentecost (Lev 23:15-22), and Tabernacles or the Feast of Booths (Lev 23:33-43). Of the three pilgrimage festivals, it can be said in passing, although not without some controversy in the scholarship, that all three underwent historical development and became associated with key events in Israel's history (de Vaux 1961:484-506).[9] While this could be contested today, I believe the following summary is still valid. The Passover was originally an agricultural festival among pastoral nomads associated with the annual sheepshearing, and came only later to commemorate the exodus from Egypt (Exod 12-13; Geoghegan 2008:147-62). The Feast of Weeks was also agricultural in origins, marking the end of wheat harvest, and although the Old Testament itself does not link it to a specific historical event, later Jewish tradition associates it with the giving of the law on Mount Sinai and covenant renewal in general (VanderKam 1992:896-97). And finally, the Feast of Tabernacles or Booths marked the final harvest of the agricultural year in the fall, marking the end of the agricultural season, and came to commemorate the wilderness sojourn (Lev 23:42-43).[10] In sum, an agricultural calendar – one held in common in the southern Levant – has become for Israel a sacred calendar commemorating YHWH's mighty acts of salvation in their past. The pilgrimage festivals have been historicized and the new historical explanations take priority over the older agricultural origins of the festivals.

Perhaps this alone would be enough to suggest ancient Israel may serve as a model for relating culture to faith. But more needs to be said here based on the rather confusing way the Old Testament marks time in its divergent calendars. We have ample evidence that early Israel shared a common calendar with their immediate neighbors, which may be called "the Canaanite-Israelite Calendar" (Cooley 2013:263-71 and 277-87). This was a luni-solar calendar (reckoning months by the moon and years by the seasons) with its beginning in the fall, and was intimately connected to the yearly agricultural and seasonal cycle. And this was only natural because of the origin and source of Israel's cultic celebrations, which as we have seen, were agricultural in nature. Then, at a point in time impossible to determine and much disputed in the scholarship, the Israelite authors created a different calendar, one based not on the agricultural nature of the traditional festivals. This calendar, sometimes called "the Sabbath Calendar" is neither completely lunar nor solar, but based instead on a 364-day cycle, being easily divisible by 7, so that any particular date in the year falls on the same day of the week every year (Cooley 2013:278-79). Rather than the moon or sun, this calendar is primarily based on the septenary Sabbath. In this way, the length of a month is disconnected from the observable lunar cycle. Month names are replaced with ordinal numbers for the 12 months, a different Hebrew term for month is used (*ḥōdeš* instead of *yeraḥ*), and the year begins in the spring rather than the fall. Some scholars have asserted that the Sabbath Calendar is "denaturalized," because it diverges from observable celestial phenomena, even while it still approximates those realities (Cooley 2013:279-81).[11] This Sabbath Calendar intentionally disconnected the Bible's method for marking time from the agricultural origins of the traditional festivals, and by putting a septenary Sabbath at the head of the festivals (Lev 23:3), it sets Sabbath observance at the center of the festival calendar unhinged from observable celestial phenomena.

The remarkable import of Gen 1:14 is instructive on these points. The opening chapter of the Bible intentionally prepares the reader for the "appointed festivals" of YHWH (Lev 23) by detailing the creation of time in Gen 1:3-5. And this merely prepares for the creation of sun, moon, and stars "for signs and for seasons and for days and years" (Gen 1:14b), setting up a trajectory for Lev 23. Time itself and the time-markers of the great sky-dome are created for the express purpose of notifying the Israelites when they must observe their sacred festivals, making the sky itself a kind of sacred, liturgical calendar (Arnold 2012:339-42). Specifically, the sun, moon, and stars were created in order to mark Israel's religious festivals (specifically for Lev 23) by providing calendrical calculations easily accessible by all Israelites. In this way, the "signs" of Gen 1:14b may refer to the festivals in general, or perhaps denote the Sabbath itself. The "seasons" denotes not the four seasons generally but specifically the festivals in the liturgical calendar. Similarly, the phrase "days and years" points to the individual days of the festivals (Lev 23:6-7,8,28) and to the Sabbath Year (Lev 25:1-7) and the Year of Jubilee (Lev 25:8-17; Arnold 2012:341-42; and compare Cooley 2013:315-16). In such a way, any significance in Israel's heritage in the West Semitic world, drawn perhaps on astral religion associated with celestial phenomena, has been transformed into a liturgical schedule for the proper worship of YHWH.

Concluding Reflections

An earlier generation of scholars overemphasized the uniqueness of Israel in the ancient world because of a theological *Tendenz* fueled by Israelite exceptionalism. Frank Moore Cross led the way in objecting to scholarship preoccupied "with the novelty of Israel's religious consciousness" and with portraying Israel as wholly discontinuous with its environment.[12] Instead, Cross insisted our work must "describe novel configurations in Israel's religion as having their origin in an orderly set of relationships which follow the usual typological sequences of historical change," and therefore must follow a consistent and valid scientific historical method. Cross led the field in a needed correction away from such preoccupation with Israelite exceptionalism.

I want to be clear that I am in no way attempting to return in this study to an overstatement of Israel's uniqueness. The twentieth century produced new data from the West Semitic world, especially from Ugarit but also from numerous archaeological finds in the southern Levant, making it impossible to argue today that ancient Israelites were anything other than completely at home among their neighbors in Syria-Palestine. At the same time, this exploration of the temple pattern, the sacrifices, and sacred festivals has highlighted significant difference, which perhaps make the comparisons worthwhile. This particular configuration addresses where, how, and when the Israelites worshiped their God, YHWH, and fits into Cross's category of "novel configurations in Israel's religion." In each case, some subtle but significant differences were introduced to religious practices. And perhaps this is precisely where Israel can serve as a model for the Church today. The distinction between form and substance may be helpful here, since formally, Israel was no different at all from its ancient Near Eastern neighbors. Similarly, cultural forms and societal norms should be no stumbling block in the Church's communication of the Gospel. But we might also suggest that Israel was substantially different from others in the ancient world, which is reflected in the pages of the Old Testament and partly explains why the Old Testament left an indelible mark on human history.

End Notes

[1] On the question of ancient Israel's distinctiveness in the ancient Near East, I cannot calculate the influence of Dr. Oswalt's teaching and scholarship on my thinking. I have also benefitted from the wisdom and anthropological insights of my colleague, Michael A. Rynkiewich, on this topic. And I wish to express here my indebtedness to my former student, Samuel Long for assistance with this article, especially for his help on the use of altars in the Levant.

[2] And see in general her pages 91-116 on "primitive worlds" for more on this.

[3] Fritz speaks specifically of the so-called "broad-room" temple structure.

[4] Especially in the Late Bronze Age and Iron I periods (Mazar 1992:169-83). For examples from one prominent city, see Robert A. Mullins (2012).

[5] The previously mentioned "inanimate objects" as idols were at times unadorned stones or wooden pillars, appearing in the Bible as *maṣṣēbâ*-stones and *'ăšērâ*-poles, and are therefore examples of "material aniconism." But Israel went a step further by insisting upon "empty-space aniconism," conceiving of God as residing over the ark and between the ark's cherubim. For definitions, see Tryggve N. D. Mettinger (1995).

[6] There was also a grain offering (Lev 2), but I am limiting this discussion simply to animal sacrifices.

[7] For the Ugaritic parallels, see Olmo Lete and Sanmartín (2003:844-45).

[8] Related to the question of the distinctiveness of Israel's sacrifices is the curious fact of Israel's blood prohibition. The food laws of Lev 11 and Deut 14 are curious enough, but they are fascinating also for their prohibition against eating carcasses (*nĕbēlâ*; Deut 14:19-20). This is most likely related to a concept of

vegetarianism, which, once lifted, needed explicit modification; hence the food laws. See Milgrom (1991:704-13, esp. 706).

[9] On the undeniable similarities between the Israelite festivals and the Hittite festival calendar, see Milgrom (2001:2076-80). Yet the historicizing descriptions of Israel's festivals in the Old Testament remain unique.

[10] For possible parallels to an Ugaritic ritual, see Olmo Lete (1999:122-23).

[11] Although Cooley believes the assertion has been overstated. The evidence suggests early Israel observed the new moon and a Shabbat day at the full moon, although the rule of rest on the seventh day was added later (Grund 2011:19-133). Perhaps the rule of rest was added at the same time as the transition to the Sabbath Calendar.

[12] Quotes in this paragraph are from Frank Moore Cross (1973: vii-viii).

WORKS CITED

Arnold, Bill T.
    2014   "Lessons of the Jerusalem Council for the Church's Debate over Sexuality." *Asbury Journal* 69:63-83.

    2012   "Genesis 1 as Holiness Preamble." Pages 331-43 in *Let us Go up to Zion: Essays in Honour of H. G. M. Williamson on the Occasion of his Sixty-Fifth Birthday*. Edited by Iain Provan and Mark J. Boda. VTSup 153. Leiden: Brill.

    2003   *1 and 2 Samuel*. The NIV Application Commentary. Grand Rapids, MI: Zondervan.

Cooley, Jeffrey L.
    2013   *Poetic Astronomy in the Ancient Near East: The Reflexes of Celestial Science in Ancient Mesopotamian, Ugaritic, and Israelite Narrative*. HACL 5. Winona Lake, IN: Eisenbrauns.

Cross, Frank Moore
    1973   *Canaanite Myth and Hebrew Epic: Essays in the History of the Religion of Israel*. Cambridge, MA: Harvard University Press.

Douglas, Mary
    2002[1966] *Purity and Danger: An Analysis of the Concepts of Pollution and Taboo*. London and New York: Routledge.

Feldman, Ron H.
    2009   "The 364-Day 'Qumran' Calendar and the Biblical Seventh-Day Sabbath: A Hypothesis Suggesting Their Simultaneous Institutionalization by Nehemiah." *Hen* 31: 342-65.

Fritz, Volkmar
    1987   "Temple Architecture: What Can Archaeology Tell Us about Solomon's Temple?" *BAR* 13: 38-49.

Geoghegan, Jeffrey
    2008   "The 'Biblical' Origins of Passover." Pages 147-62 in *Sacred History, Sacred Literature: Essays on Ancient Israel, the Bible, and Religion in Honor of R. E. Friedman on his Sixtieth Birthday*. Edited by Shawna Dolansky. Winona Lake, IN: Eisenbrauns.

Grund, Alexandra
    2011   *Die Entstehung des Sabbats: Seine Bedeutung für Israels Zeitkonzept und Erinnerungskultur*. FAT 75. Tübingen: Mohr Siebeck.

Hallo, William W.
    1987   "The Origins of the Sacrificial Cult: New Evidence from Mesopotamia and Israel." Pages 3-13 in *Ancient Israelite Religion: Essays in Honor of Frank Moore Cross*. Edited by Patrick D. Miller, Jr., Paul D. Hanson, and S. Dean McBride. Philadelphia: Fortress Press.

Haran, Menahem
    1985   *Temples and Temple-Service in Ancient Israel: An Inquiry into Biblical Cult Phenomena and the Historical Setting of the Priestly School*. Winona Lake, IN: Eisenbrauns.

Hundley, Michael B.
    2013   *Gods in Dwellings: Temples and Divine Presence in the Ancient Near East*. SBLWAW 3. Atlanta, GA: Society of Biblical Literature.

Kellermann, Diether
    2001   "עוֹלָה/עֹלָה" Pages 96-113 in *Theological Dictionary of the Old Testament*. Edited by G. Johannes Botterweck, Helmer Ringgren, and Heinz-Josef Fabry. Translated by David E. Green. Volume 11. Grand Rapids, MI: Eerdmans.

Mazar, Amihai
1992 "Temples of the Middle and Late Bronze Ages and the Iron Age." Pages 161-87 in *The Architecture of Ancient Israel: From the Prehistoric to the Persian Periods: In Memory of Immanuel (Munya) Dunayevsky.* Edited by Aharon Kempinski and Ronny Reich. Jerusalem: Israel Exploration Society.

Mettinger, Tryggve N. D.
1995 *No Graven Image? Israelite Aniconism in Its Ancient Near Eastern Context.* ConBOT 42. Stockholm: Almqvist & Wiksell International.

Milgrom, Jacob
2001 *Leviticus 23-27: A New Translation with Introduction and Commentary.* AB 3B. New York: Doubleday.

1991 *Leviticus 1-16: A New Translation with Introduction and Commentary.* AB 3. New York: Doubleday.

Mullins, Robert A.
2012 "The Late Bronze and Iron Age Temples at Beth-Shean." Pages 127-57 in *Temple Building and Temple Cult: Architecture and Cultic Paraphernalia of Temples in the Levant (2.-1. Mill. B.C.E.).* Edited by Jens Kamlah and Henrike Michelau. ADPV 41. Wiesbaden: Harrassowitz.

Nielsen, Kjeld
1986 *Incense in Ancient Israel.* VTSup 38. Leiden: E.J. Brill.

Olmo Lete, Gregorio del
1999 *Canaanite Religion according to the Liturgical Texts of Ugarit.* Bethesda, MD: CDL Press.

Olmo Lete, Gregorio del, and Joaquín Sanmartín
2003 *A Dictionary of the Ugaritic Language in the Alphabetic Tradition.* 2 vols. Handbook of Oriental Studies Section 1, The Near and Middle East 67. Leiden and Boston: Brill.

Oswalt, John N.
    2009   *The Bible among The Myths: Unique Revelation or Just Ancient Literature?* Grand Rapids, MI: Zondervan.

VanderKam, James C.
    1992   "Weeks, Festival of." Pages 895-97 in *Anchor Bible Dictionary.* Edited by David Noel Freedman. Volume 6. New York: Doubleday.

Vaux, Roland de
    1961   *Ancient Israel: Its Life and Institutions.* Translated by J. McHugh. New York: McGraw-Hill.

A Prophet Like Moses? Who or Why?

Daniel I. Block

Keywords:

prophet, Moses, Deuteronomy 18:9-22, diviner, messiah

Daniel I. Block (DPhil, School of Archaeology and Oriental Studies, University of Liverpool) is the Gunther H. Knoedler Professor Emeritus of Old Testament at Wheaton College.

ABSTRACT

This paper examines the Hebrew understanding of Moses' statement about a "a prophet like me" that YHWH would raise up in Deuteronomy 18:15. Here it is examined within its larger context of verses 9–22, with a comparison of the prophetic role of Moses held up against the role of diviners and fortune-tellers in other regional religious traditions. The role of this scripture for a Jewish understanding of future prophets is highlighted as opposed to any messianic interpretation of the text.

INTRODUCTION

It is a little more than fifteen years since I first expressed publicly my preliminary interpretation of Moses' anticipation of "a prophet like me" (נָבִיא כָּמֹנִי) whom YHWH would raise up (Deut 18:15; Block 2003:26–32). Although the messianic interpretation of this text has a long history,[1] the context in which it is embedded relates directly to a subject that has long interested my dear friend, John Oswalt, in whose honor I submit this essay. Deuteronomy 18:9–22 is of critical importance in assessing the difference between the experimental and tenuous nature of pagan religions of First Testament times and the revelatory nature of Israel's faith. John's particular interest in this subject has been forcefully argued in his volume, *The Bible among The Myths: Unique Revelation or Just Ancient Literature?* (Grand Rapids, MI: Zondervan, 2009:185–94). My intention here is not to revisit what John has done with the notion of revelation in general, but to examine what this passage has to say about the matter, and then make a few observations on whether the passage itself supports a messianic interpretation. What is striking about the messianic approach is the inattention of defenders of this view to contextual, literary, rhetorical, and discourse grammatical features of Deut 18:9–22 (Jones 2014).[2]

THE LITERARY CONTEXT OF DEUTERONOMY 18:9–22

Within Moses' third address (12:1–26:10; 28:1–69) Deut 18:9–22 concludes a more or less self-contained unit involving instructions concerning administrative and religious officials that extends from 16:18 to 18:22. Indeed, if we focus on the officers in the larger unit, we observe a chiastic structure:

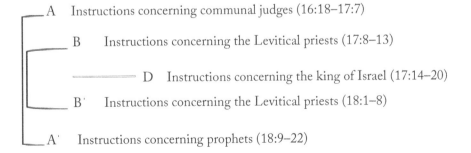

A   Instructions concerning communal judges (16:18–17:7)

    B   Instructions concerning the Levitical priests (17:8–13)

        D   Instructions concerning the king of Israel (17:14–20)

    B'   Instructions concerning the Levitical priests (18:1–8)

A'   Instructions concerning prophets (18:9–22)

Scholars commonly interpret this section of Deuteronomy as a sort of administrative constitution for Israel (Halpern 1981:226–33; Rütersworden 1987:89–90; McBride 1987:229–44; Nelson 2002:212). However, there is no evidence that these laws ever existed separately, apart from their incorporation into the book (McConville 2002:281). Furthermore, this approach overloads these sections with undue political freight, at the expense of more central issues, which are spiritual and religious. On first sight the opening statement ("Judges and officers you may/shall appoint in all your towns," 16:18) seems to focus on the leaders, and invites us to expect instructions on how they were to execute their judicial functions (cf. 1:16–18).[3] But there is no shift in addressee from the previous section, as Moses insists that the pursuit of righteousness is everybody's business.

This trajectory carries on throughout this section. None of the officials (judges, kings, priests, prophets) are addressed directly. For the people's benefit, in 17:14–20 the focus is entirely on the king's role as a model of covenant righteousness as spelled out in "this Torah"; not a word is said of his performance of normal royal duties. Deuteronomy 18:1–8 says even less about priestly obligations within the social and administrative structures; instead the emphasis is on the Israelites' responsibilities to care for those whom YHWH chose to stand before him. A primary function of 18:9–22 is to clarify the role of the prophet of YHWH in Israel's pursuit of righteousness and to assist the people in discriminating between true and false prophets, so that they might carry out the policies required in 13:1–5[Heb 2–6].

Throughout Deut 16:18–18:22, the predominant concern is not merely "social justice" (מִשְׁפָּט), but righteousness in all its dimensions, demonstrated especially in the people's absolute fidelity to YHWH. Deuteronomy 16:20 provides the key to this entire section: צֶדֶק צֶדֶק תִּרְדֹּף, "Righteousness, righteousness you shall pursue." What follows is not a manual for judges, kings, priests, and prophets, but instructions for the people, particularly male heads of households, on the place of these officials in the maintenance of the nation's righteousness. This includes the instructions concerning the prophet in 18:9–22.

THE STYLE AND STRUCTURE OF DEUT. 18:9–22

Robert Dooley and Stephen Levinsohn have observed that the starting point of a new literary unit is often marked by a "preposed expression, especially one of time" (2001:40). In Deuteronomy, the signal is often the particle כִּי, followed by an imperfect verb, which sets the temporal context for what follows.[4] The כִּי clause in

18:9a signals a transition from the discussion of the people's responsibilities toward Levitical priests (vv. 1–8) to YHWH's provision for ongoing communication with his people through a prophet (vv. 9–22).

An examination of the text that follows rightly begins with a consideration of its discourse grammar. Like most others, in an earlier treatment I identified three sub-units in this passage, consisting of verses 9–14, 15–20, and 21–22 respectively (Block 2012:434–38). However, upon closer attention to the discourse logic and grammar, verse 14 is best interpreted as the introduction to verses 15–20.[5] On the surface, verse 14 appears to summarize verses 9–13 exhibiting a similar A B structure, with A describing the practices of the nations and B demanding a different paradigm of revelatory communication from the Israelites (Table 1). The introductory particle כִּי in verses 12a and 14a seems to reinforce this approach.

Table 1: The Parallel Structures of Deuteronomy 18:9–13 and 14

When you come to the land that YHWH your God is giving you, you shall not learn to act according to the despicable behavior of those nations. There shall not be found among you anyone who passes his son or his daughter in the fire, who practices divination, or who tells fortunes, or who interprets omens, or who is a sorcerer, or a charmer, or who is a medium, an occultist, or one who inquires of the dead, because all who do these things are an abomination to YHWH, and because of these abominations YHWH your God is driving them out before you.	Assuredly, these nations, which you are about to dispossess, listen to fortune-tellers and to diviners.
You shall be blameless before YHWH your God.	But as for you, YHWH your God has not granted to you [permission] to do this.

However, several factors argue against this interpretation. First, and most obviously, in the Masoretic formatting the *setumah* (ס) inserted between verses 13 and 14 suggests the rabbis saw something that scholars often miss. Second, the כִּי particles at the beginning of verses 12 and 14 obviously function differently. In the first instance כִּי introduces a causal clause, an interpretation that is confirmed by the following differently constructed clause (v. 12c). In the second the כִּי functions deictically and assertively (Follingstad 2001:568), introducing a paradigm that replaces and corrects what precedes.[6] Third, this interpretation is reinforced by the emphatic fronting of וְאַתָּה ("But as for you"), in 14c, which corresponds to the fronting of הַגּוֹיִם הָאֵלֶּה ("these nations") in 14a, and intentionally forbids the Israelites from resorting to divination and sorcery. Fourth, the repetition of the verb שָׁמַע ("to hear, listen") in 14a and 15b binds verses 14 and 15 inextricably and highlights the intended contrast and replacement motif; whereas the nations listen to fortune-tellers and diviners, Israelites are to listen to the prophet like Moses, whom YHWH will raise up. The awkward but parallel construction of these sentences, with the verbs as the last element, strengthens the rhetorical intent:

כִּי הַגּוֹיִם הָאֵלֶּה [אֲשֶׁר אַתָּה יוֹרֵשׁ אוֹתָם] . . . . אֶל־מְעֹנְנִים וְאֶל־קֹסְמִים יִשְׁמָעוּ

וְאַתָּה [לֹא כֵן נָתַן לְךָ יְהוָה אֱלֹהֶיךָ: נָבִיא מִקִּרְבְּךָ מֵאַחֶיךָ כָּמֹנִי יָקִים לְךָ יְהוָה אֱלֹהֶיךָ] אֵלָיו . . . . . . תִּשְׁמָעוּן

Assuredly, <u>these nations</u> . . . . to fortune-tellers and to diviners <u>they listen.</u>
  <u>But as for you,</u> . . . . to him [the prophet]   <u>you must listen.</u>

Having deprived the Israelites of pagan forms of divination, verses 14–15 together introduce them to YHWH's graciously provided alternative. Through the institution of prophecy YHWH will satisfy the impulses that drive other peoples to their abhorrent (תּוֹעֵבָה) magical practices.[7] While he denies them one widely perceived benefit—access to supernatural knowledge via mediums—he replaces it with another more reliable gift: access to himself via clear revelation through a prophet. In so doing he fleshes out what "blameless" (תָּמִים) communication with YHWH (cf. v. 13) looks like.

Having established that verse 14 introduces a new subsection, which carries on through the divine speech in verses 17b–20, the next discourse marker of a literary break occurs in verse 21a. The transition is signaled by וְכִי ("Now") and the change to a verb with a second person subject, "you." Following a rhetorical strategy that is common in the book, Moses' own voice returns to introduce a hypothetical interlocutor, who expresses verbally how the Israelites might respond in the future to competing claims to the office of prophet and the practice of the prophetic vocation.[8] Here he builds on chapter 13, where appealing to people to go after other gods is one of the marks of a false prophet (13:2–6[Heb 1–5]). Now Moses focuses on predictive prophecy, which is the primary goal of the pagan divinatory practices listed in verses 10–11 and 14. That Moses should refer to people who (falsely) claim to speak for YHWH speaks to the ubiquity of fraudulent prophetic utterances in the ancient Near East.[9] It will obviously not suffice for a so-called prophet to preface, punctuate, or end a declaration with one of the common prophetic formulas, such as the citation formula (כֹּה אָמַר אֲדֹנָי יהוה, "Thus has

Adonay YHWH declared") or the divine signatory formula (נְאֻם אֲדֹנָי יהוה, "the declaration of Adonay YHWH").[10]

THE IDENTITY AND FUNCTION OF THE PROPHET DEUTERONOMY 18:14–20

Having established the literary and cultural context for Deut 18:9–22 it remains to examine more carefully verses 15–19, to see what light they might shed on the identity and role of the prophet like Moses.

First, the opening temporal clause in verse 9 points to (the beginning of) the fulfillment of the promise of the prophet in the near future; it does no good to promise an eschatological figure when the temptation of pagan divination is just ahead: "When you enter the land." The form of the beginning links this pericope with the instructions concerning the king: "When you enter the land and possess it and live in it (17:14).

Second, the medium of divine revelation is called a נָבִיא. The word was encountered earlier in 13:2 [Heb 1], in association with חֹלֵם חֲלוֹם, "dreamer of dreams." Although the First Testament refers to prophets by several designations,[11] נָבִיא is the most common. The etymology of this word remains uncertain, but it seems best to the interpret the form as an I-class passive of a hypothetical root, נָבָא, "to call,"[12] hence "one summoned by God."[13] Although some have understood the use of the singular נָבִיא, rather than the plural נְבִיאִים, to refer to a specific future prophet, nothing in this context points in that direction. Rather, the singular should be understood something like a prophet in each generation (Perlitt 1971:596; Mayes 1981:282; Nelson 2002:228). Moses hereby assures the people that they will never need to resort to manipulative divination, because YHWH will provide for a succession of prophets, all of whom will command obedience.

Third, the prophet will be divinely chosen and installed. The verb הֵקִים, meaning "to raise up" and entrust with a commission, is used elsewhere of divinely appointed saviors (מוֹשִׁיעִים, Judg 3:9, 15), tribal chieftains (שֹׁפְטִים, Judg 2:16, 18), a king (מֶלֶךְ 1 Kings 14:14), a priest כֹּהֵן, (1 Sam 2:35), sentries (צֹפִים, Jer 6:17), and shepherds (רֹעִים, Jer 23:4; Ezek 34:23; Zech 11:16). In the broader context of Deut 16:18–18:22, the direct appointment and installation by YHWH of the prophet represents a contrast to the judges and officials (שֹׁפְטִים וְשֹׁטְרִים), whom the people are to appoint (נָתַן) in all their towns when they have crossed the Jordan (16:18), and the king, whom YHWH will choose but whom the people will install (שִׂים in 17:15; הֵקִים in 28:36). Like the perfect verb form הֵקִים in Judges 2:18, here we should interpret the imperfect יָקִים in a distributive sense, referring not to a single appointment but to a series, that is, from time to time as needed.[14] This accords generally with the concern in 16:18–18:22 with administrative and religious offices and institutions, and more particularly with the instructions concerning the king in 17:12–20.

Fourth, this prophet will be raised up "from the midst" (מִקִּרְבְּךָ) and "from the brotherhood" (מֵאַחֶיךָ) of Israel. He will come from the same pool of candidates as the king (17:15). Since the one "from the midst of your brothers"[15] had been contrasted with "a foreigner" (אִישׁ נָכְרִי) as recently as 17:15, there is no need to specify more closely what is meant. By highlighting the Israelite origin of the prophet, Moses may have had in mind Balaam, the prophet for hire from Mesopotamia whom the Moabites had engaged to curse Israel (cf. 23:4–5; Num 22–24). Since the prophet like Moses will be raised up from within Israel, he will have nothing in common with the diviners and magicians now in the land. In contrast to the kings, whom Gen 49:10 specifies as coming from the tribe of Judah, and the priestly functionaries, who are all Levites (17:9, 18; 18:1; 24:8; 27:9), the promise leaves open both the tribal source and the gender of prophets who will succeed Moses.

Fifth, this prophet will be like Moses. Grammatically כָּמֹנִי ("like me") functions as an attributive modifier of נָבִיא, "prophet," that is, the one whom YHWH will raise up will be a prophet after the order of Moses (cf. Schüle 2001:118). As if to reinforce Moses' role as "mouthpiece" of YHWH, verse 18 puts the promise of a prophet into YHWH's own mouth and presents it as a benefit for the people that YHWH had made to Moses at Horeb. Except for some adjustments in word order and the shift from third to first person, YHWH's words in verse 18a largely repeat what Moses had expressed in verse 15 (Table 2).

Table 2: Moses' and YHWH's Promises of a Prophet Like Moses

Verse 15	Verse 18
נָבִיא מִקִּרְבְּךָ מֵאַחֶיךָ כָּמֹנִי יָקִים לְךָ יְהוָה אֱלֹהֶיךָ	נָבִיא אָקִים לָהֶם מִקֶּרֶב אֲחֵיהֶם כָּמוֹךָ
A prophet from your midst, from your kinsfolk like me he will raise up for you YHWH your God.	A prophet I will raise up for them from the midst of your kinsfolk like you

The prophetic institution receives surprisingly little attention in the Pentateuch. Indeed, the word נָבִיא appears only four times prior to Deut 13 (Gen 20:7; Exod 7:1; Num 11:25–26; 12:6–8), and the cognate verb only twice (Num 11:25–26). Of these Num 12:6–8 is most remarkable, because it explicitly contrasts Moses' role with that of prophets. Responding to Miriam and Aaron's claim that they had as much right to speak for YHWH as Moses did, God declared that even if they were prophets, their status was inferior to that of Moses. Whereas he (YHWH) speaks to prophets through visions and dreams, he speaks to Moses directly ("mouth to mouth"), clearly (מַרְאֶה) and unambiguously (לֹא בְחִידֹת, "not in riddles"). This paradigm of Mosaic prophecy suits the present context, which uses as a foil the divination of the nations, which is typically indirect, obscure, and ambiguous (cf. Block 2005).

Verses 16–20 clarify what Moses means by a prophet "like me." First, the holders of this office will be as inspired as Moses was: as YHWH had done to Moses, so he will do for his successor(s): he will put his words in their mouths (v. 18b). Second, they will have the same commission Moses had: they shall declare the word of YHWH to the people (v. 18c–d). Third, they will come with the same authority as Moses: they will speak in the name of YHWH (v. 19c). Fourth, they will come with the same guarantee: YHWH will not leave it to them to secure the proper response of the audience; he will personally hold the latter accountable for rejecting the prophets' message (v. 19a). Although Moses reported this divine speech as having been addressed to him at Horeb (cf. v. 16a–b), as he recalled that moment on the Plains of Moab forty years later he may have had in mind his own siblings' challenge to his authority; YHWH personally called them to account (Num 12:1–15).

In verse 20 YHWH digresses to reinforce this image of a prophet like Moses and describe a hypothetical prophet who is not like Moses: he speaks presumptuously without YHWH's authorization to speak in his name; he declares a word that YHWH has not put in his mouth; and he speaks in the name of another deity. According to verses 21–22 the proof of a true prophet is that his prediction is always fulfilled.[16]

These comparisons with Moses speak only to the nature of true prophecy. They do not mean that all subsequent prophets—or an eschatological ideal or messianic figure—would be clones of Moses. Rather, in the narrator's eulogy on Moses he declared unequivocally his uniqueness within the historical succession of prophets:[10]

> Never since has there arisen a prophet in Israel like Moses, whom YHWH knew face to face. He was unequaled for all the signs and wonders that YHWH sent him to perform in the land of Egypt, against Pharaoh and all his servants and his entire land, and for all the mighty deeds and all the terrifying displays of power that Moses performed in the sight of all Israel. (Deut 34:10–12, NRSV modified).

Contrary to some, there is no need to date this epitaph to the exile or to the post-exilic period, after Israel's prophetic institution had been shut down (Sailhamer 1993:31; Rydelnik 2010:61; Kim 1995:276–82). It only requires enough time for the appearance of several representatives, which is possible if one posits a date for the composition of the book of Deuteronomy more or less as we have it (and the Pentateuch as a whole) to the United Monarchy period (as I do). And whether one interprets וְלֹא־קָם . . . עֹוד as "never since" (NRSV), "since then" (NIV, NASB; cf. ESV), "never again" (NJPS), or the entire clause as "No prophet like Moses ever came" (Sailhamer 1995:247–48; Rydelnik 2010:62–63), this comment recognizes that even if Moses was the founder and paradigm of the entire line of true Israelite prophets, for his intimacy with YHWH (cf. Num 12:6–8), his performance of signs and wonders,[17] his mighty demonstrations of power (הַחֲזָקָה הַיָּד), and all his awesome deeds (כֹּל הַמֹּורָא הַגָּדֹול), he was in a class of his own. But this need not mean there have been no prophets like Moses in other respects. While the expression "like Moses" (כְּמֹשֶׁה) in 34:10 links this text to 18:15 and 18, in no way does it suggest either the failure or nonfulfillment of YHWH's and Moses' predictions of a prophet like Moses in Israel's past, or invite them to look forward to a new Messianic "Moses" who would speak with God face to face.[18] To claim this text as support for the view that the Torah points to a future Messiah is both gratuitous and tendentious. This image is entirely in the eye of the beholder, and represents the result of forcing evidence to suit a conclusion pre-established on other grounds.

Conclusion

The foregoing discussion represents a modest foray into a subject that cannot be resolved in one short essay. However, in my assessment neither the present context nor any other First Testament text offers any support for interpreting Deut 18:14–19 messianically, either in its expectation of a singular eschatological prophetic Messiah or in its anticipation of an ideal Prophet at the end of a succession of prophets. The point of this text is not to satisfy the preoccupation of later interpreters—Christian or otherwise—to find predictions of the Messiah in the Pentateuch, but to reassure Moses' immediate hearers and those who would hear his Torah read every seven years at the Festival of Sukkoth/Booths (Deut 31:9–13), that YHWH would continue to reveal himself and his will to them through prophets like Moses. The specific search for *who* this prophet might be is misguided. In fact, the characterization of the prophet like Moses applies to all subsequent true prophets, including Paul.[19]

END NOTES

[1] For a short survey of this approach and a more sustained critique, see Daniel I. Block, "A Prophet Like Moses: Another Look at Deuteronomy 18:9–22," in *The Triumph of Grace: Literary and Theological Studies in Deuteronomy and Deuteronomic Themes* (Eugene, OR: Wipf & Stock), forthcoming.

[2] For a helpful examination of the discourse grammar of this passage, see Jones, "Reconsidering the *Prophetengesetz*." The following textlinguistic discussion is indebted to Jones.

[3] Unless otherwise indicated, all translations of biblical texts are my own.

[4] E.g. Deut 4:25; 7:1; 12:20, 29; 17:14; 18:9; 19:1 20:1, 10, 19; 21:10; 22:8; 23:10[Heb 9]; 24:10, 19; 26:12. In 18:21 the form is וְכִי, signaling the beginning of a new paragraph, though the topic continues to be the prophet and his message.

[5] See also Jones ("Reconsidering the *Prophetengesetz*"), with a more detailed discussion.

[6] Following Jones, "Reconsidering the *Prophetengesetz*." On the use of כִּי to signal "modification of active information by replacement and correction," see Follingstad, *Deictic Viewpoint*, 561.

[7] Labuschagne (*Deuteronomium*, 134) rightly argues for a fundamental difference between prophets, who proclaim the word of YHWH, and diviners, who predict the future. But these differences do not rule out similarities. For further discussion on the relationship between Israelite prophecy and divination see Overholt, *Channels of Prophecy*, 117–47; Barstad, "No Prophets," 47–49. On the relationship between prophecy and ecstasy, see the still helpful study by Haller, *Charisma und Ekstasis*, 5–39.

⁸ As in 7:17; 8:17; and 9:4, here the interlocutor happens to be talking to himself. The idiom, תֹּאמַר בִּלְבָבֶךָ, "you say in your heart," is euphemistic for "you think."

⁹ Cf. Jer 23:16–22; Ezek 13:21–13:16.

¹⁰ On these and other divine speech markers used by prophets, see Block, *Ezekiel Chapters 1–24*, 32–36.

¹¹ רֹאִים, "seer"; חֹזִים, "visionary"; עַבְדֵי יהוה, "servants of YHWH"; מַלְאֲכֵי יהוה. "messengers/envoys of YHWH"; אִישׁ הָאֱלֹהִים, "man of God".

¹² Cognate to Akkadian *nabû(m)*, "to call, name." *AHw*, 697b, 699b. The verb occurs in the Old Testament only in the reflexive stems (niphal, hithpael). *HALOT*, 659.

¹³ Analogous to many other official terms: מָשִׁיַח, "anointed one, messiah"; נָגִיד, "promoted one, ruler"; נָשִׂיא, "raised one, prince"; נָזִיר, "consecrated one, Nazirite"; פָּקִיד, "appointed one, overseer"; שָׂכִיר, "hired one, hireling." For a defense of this interpretation of נָבִיא and a discussion of such forms, see John Huehnergard, "On the Etymology and Meaning of Hebrew *nābi´*," *ErIsr* 26 (1999): 88*–93*. Cf. Daniel E. Fleming ("The Etymological Origins of the Hebrew *nābi´*: The One Who Invokes God." *CBQ* 55 [1993]:217–24), who argues for an active meaning, "one who invokes the gods."

¹⁴ Cf. Rashi, who saw in this text the promise of a succession of prophets (לנביא מנביא). See further Chiesa, "La Promessa di un Profeta (Deut 18,15-20)," *BO* 15 (1973) :17–26, esp. 20–23. Contra Yoon-Hee Kim, "The 'Prophet Like Moses' : Deut 18 :15-22 Reexamined within the Context of the Pentateuch and in Light of the Final Shape of the TaNaK" (PhD diss., Trinity Evangelical Divinity School, 1995), 89–94.

¹⁵ Note the stylistic variations in these two passages: 17:15, מִקֶּרֶב אַחֶיךָ, "from the midst of your brothers"; 18:15, מִקִּרְבְּךָ מֵאַחֶיךָ, "from your midst from your brothers."

[16] The narrative of Saul's consultation of the woman of Endor and the appearance of the prophet Samuel from the netherworld in 1 Sam 28:3–25 reinforces my insistence that this text focuses on YHWH's promised prophetic alternative to pagan means of communicating with the divine, and on the importance of future generations listening to those who speak for YHWH, rather than on the identity of some future eschatological prophet. For explorations of the relationship between this text and Deut 18:9–22, see Bill T. Arnold, "Necromancy and Cleromancy in 1 and 2 Samuel," *CBQ* 66 (2004): 199–213; Joshua Berman, "The Legal Blend in Biblical Narrative (Joshua 20:1–9, Judges 6:25–31, 1 Samuel 15:2, 28:3–25, 2 Kings 4:1–7, Jeremiah 34:12–17, Nehemiah 5:1–12)," JBL 134 (2015): 117–21.

[17] Remarkably this is the only place in Deuteronomy where הָאֹתֹת וְהַמּוֹפְתִים, "the signs and wonders" are attributed to Moses; elsewhere they are always portrayed as divine acts. See 4:34; 6:22; 7:19; 11:3; 26:8; 29:3 [Heb 2].

[18] Contra Rydelnik, *Messianic Hope*, 63–64.

[19] Elsewhere I have argued that in the first chapter of Galatians, Paul deliberately characterizes himself as a prophet in the long succession founded by Moses. See Daniel I. Block, "Hearing Galatians with Moses: An Examination of Paul as a Second and Seconding Moses," in *The Triumph of Grace*, forthcoming.

WORKS CITED

Barstad, Hans M.
   1993   "No Prophets? Recent Developments in Biblical Prophetic Research and Ancient Near Eastern Prophecy." *Journal for the Study of the Old Testament* 57: 39–60.

Block, Daniel I.
   2017   "A Prophet Like Moses: Another Look at Deuteronomy 18:9–22 and the History of Its Interpretation." Forthcoming in *The Triumph of Grace: Literary and Theological Studies in Deuteronomy and Deuteronomic Themes* (Eugene, OR: Wipf & Stock).

   "Hearing Galatians with Moses: An Examination of Paul as a Second and Seconding Moses." In *Sepher Torath Mosheh: Studies in the Composition and Interpretation of Deuteronomy*, edited by Daniel I. Block and Richard L. Schultz. Peabody, MA: Hendrickson, forthcoming.

   2012   *Deuteronomy*, NIVAC. Grand Rapids: Zondervan.

   2005   "What has Delphi to do with Samaria? Ambiguity and Delusion in Israelite Prophecy." In *Writing and Ancient Near Eastern Society: Papers in Honour of Alan R. Millard*. Ed. P. Bienkowski, C. Mee, and E. Slater, 189–216. New York/London: T & T Clark.

   2003   "My Servant David: Ancient Israel's Vision of the Messiah." In *Israel's Messiah in the Bible and the Dead Sea Scrolls*, edited by R. S. Hess and M. D. Carroll R., 17–56. Grand Rapids: Baker.

   1997   *The Book of Ezekiel Chapters 1–24*. NICOT. Grand Rapids: Eerdmans, 1997.

Chiesa, B.
   1973   "La Promessa di un Profeta (Deut 18,15–20)." *Bibliotheca Orientalis* 15: 17–26.

Dooley, Robert A., and Stephen H. Levinsohn
    2001   *Analyzing Discourse: A Manual of Basic Concepts*. Dallas, TX: SIL International.

Fleming, Daniel E.
    1993   "The Etymological Origins of the Hebrew *nābîʾ*: The One Who Invokes God." *Catholic Biblical Quarterly* 55: 217–24.

Follingstad, Carl Martin
    2001   *Deictic Viewpoint in Biblical Hebrew Text: A Syntagmatic and Paradigmatic Analysis of the Particle* כי. Dallas, TX: SIL International.

Haller, Eduard
    1960   *Charisma und Ekstasis: Die Erzählung von dem Propheten Micha ben Imlah 1. Kön. 22,1–28a*. Theologische Existenz Heute 82. Munich: Chr. Kaiser.

Halpern, Baruch
    1981   *The Constitution of the Monarchy in Israel*. HSM 25. Chico, CA: Scholars Press.

Huehnergard, J.
    1999   "On the Etymology and Meaning of Hebrew *nābîʾ*." *Eretz Israel* 26: 88*–93*.

Jones, Jennifer B.
    2014   "Reconsidering the *Prophetengesetz*: A Text Linguistic Approach to Deuteronomy 18:9–22. Unpublished seminar paper, Wheaton College.

Kim, Yoon-Hee
    1995   "The 'Prophet Like Moses': Deut 18:15–22 Reexamined within the Context of the Pentateuch and in Light of the Final Shape of the TaNaK." Ph.D. diss. Trinity Evangelical Divinity School.

Labuschagne, C. J.
1990   *Deuteronomium.* 2 parts. De Prediking van het Oude Testament. Nijkerk: Uitgeverij Callenbach.

Mayes, A. D. H.
1981   *Deuteronomy.* New Century Bible. Grand Rapids: Eerdmans.

McBride, S. Dean
1987   "The Polity of the Covenant People: The Book of Deuteronomy." *Interpretation* 41: 229–44.

McConville, J. G.
2002   *Deuteronomy.* Apollos Old Testament Commentary. Downers Grove: InterVarsity.

Nelson, Richard D.
2002   *Deuteronomy: A Commentary.* OTL. Louisville: Westminster John Knox.

Oswalt, John N.
2009   *The Bible among The Myths: Unique Revelation or Just Ancient Literature?* Grand Rapids, MI: Zondervan.

Overholt, Thomas W.
1989   *Channels of Prophecy: The Social Dynamics of Prophetic Activity.* Minneapolis: Fortress.

Perlitt, Lothar
1971   "Mose als Prophet." *Evangelische Theologie* 31: 588–608.

Rüterswörden, U.
1987   *Von der politischen Gemeinschaft zur Gemeinde: Studien zu Dt 16,18–18,22.* BBB 65. Frankfurt-am-Main: Athenäum.

Rydelnik, Michael
    2010   *The Messianic Hope: Is the Hebrew Bible Really Messianic?* NAC Studies in Bible and Theology. Nashville: Broadman & Holman.

Sailhamer, John H.
    1995   *Introduction to Old Testament Theology: A Canonical Approach.* Grand Rapids: Zondervan.

    1993   "The Canon of the Hebrew Bible: A Wisdom Redaction?" Paper presented to the Society of Biblical Literature, Washington, D.C., November.

Schüle, Andreas
    2001   "Kāmokā—der Nächste wie Du. Zur Philologie des Liebesgebotes von Lev 19,18.34," *Kleine Untersuchungen zur Sprache des Alten Testaments un seiner Umwelt* 2: 97–129.

Seeing Double: An Iconographic Reading of Genesis 2-3

ancient Near East, iconography, visual literacy, Adam and Eve Seal

Christina Bosserman is a PhD student at The Catholic University of America.

ABSTRACT

This paper examines the role of visual literacy in the construction of biblical narrative, by asking how visual images in the ancient Near East might have been understood by biblical writers and how these understandings (or misunderstandings) may have influenced the development of the biblical text. In particular, the issue of visual illiteracy is examined in light of Mesopotamian seals with images similar to the Garden of Eden story found in Genesis 2-3, and how these visual images might have resulted in the confusion of one or two trees in the center of the Garden.

INTRODUCTION

Pastors and teachers of scripture will undoubtedly encounter the abundance of similarities between Israel and her neighbors, whether from a simple observation that YHWH brings rain like Baal (Psalm 29), or through many years studying the texts and archaeological discoveries that demonstrate over and over again that Israel is culturally at home with her neighbors. In one of his more recent books, *The Bible Among the Myths*, Dr. John Oswalt (2009:92) says that when we encounter similarities, we should not therefore conclude, "Hebrew religion is just a variant of the general west Semitic religion of its day." Oswalt (2009:13-14) challenges evolutionary explanations of Israel's religious worldview *vis-à-vis* her neighbors, arguing that while similarities between Israel's religion and her ancient Near Eastern counterparts abound, many of those similarities are "accidental" (a feature "not essential to that object's being"), while the underlying differences often not observed on the surface are in fact the "essentials" (if removed the thing will "cease to be itself"). What appears to be superficially the "same" betrays contrasting worldviews about the divine-human relationship when analyzed at a conceptual level.[1] Oswalt's argument principally resides in the comparison of the Hebrew scriptures with non-Israelite texts from the same periods.

Another entry into this discussion is through iconography, the study of ancient Near Eastern visual materials. Like comparative studies of written texts, iconographic research engages visual material produced in multiple ancient Near Eastern contexts and brings such study to bear on both Israelite and non-Israelite written materials.[2] When the nexus of biblical text and ancient Near Eastern image is in view, questions relevant to Oswalt's scholarship emerge: did the producers of Israelite texts share the worldview that produced similar non-Israelite images? When a biblical text employs visual subjects such as water, trees, and divine figures, are those similarities "accidental" or "essential" to the meaning of the biblical text? Or, to put it in the terms explored in this paper, are biblical texts "literate" or "illiterate" in regards to the meaning of non-Israelite iconography?

As it relates to visual and textual borrowing by Israelite authors from their non-Israelite neighbors, a valuable starting point for scholarship is a humble one; one cannot reliably understand the conceptual world of ancient cultures without significant research, an endeavor worth the rigors of an entire career. However, this humility often accompanies a further assumption: that by nature of their chronological and geographic proximity, ancient Near Eastern cultures understood each other. Therefore, when a borrowing is observed, the natural trajectory is to treat the ancient borrowing as a valid reflection of the conceptual world of the source culture. This is a common starting point for studies on iconographic motifs present in the Hebrew Bible and vice versa.[3] Such studies have made a tremendous contribution to our understanding of biblical texts in their ancient Near Eastern contexts, and clearly there is merit in such a starting point for iconographic study. The question I wish to explore with this essay is whether there is evidence in the Hebrew Bible that, at least occasionally, authors of texts were "iconographically illiterate"? Or, to pose the question in another way, is it possible to detect evidence that a biblical author has reflected a foreign visual motif in such a way that betrays little or no knowledge of its indigenous conceptual context? I will enter this discussion with a frequently cited example of *modern* iconographic illiteracy – the so-called *Adam and Eve seal* and its intersections with the biblical text of Genesis 2-3. Further discussion will consider first whether a case can be made from the text of Genesis that a foreign iconographic motif has informed its author. And second, can Genesis 2-3 be described as "literate" of the iconography's conceptual and/or mythic context? Towards an answer to this question, this essay will consider the text itself, the issue of proximity as it relates to visual and cultural exchange, applicable contributions from the social scientific field of visual literacy, and other biblical scholars who have offered similar arguments from textual evidence.

THE ADAM AND EVE SEAL AS AN EXAMPLE OF ICONOGRAPHIC ILLITERACY

The so-called *Adam and Eve Seal* (see Figure One) as it is titled by the British Museum likely got its nickname from its apparent "illustration" of Genesis 2-3, but also from one of its earliest interpreters, George Smith (1876:90-91), who after viewing the seal concluded that "it is evident that a form of the story of the Fall, similar to that of Genesis, was known in early times in Babylonia."[4] The Museum describes the scene as follows: "a female figure with her hair in a bun holds out her left hand and sits facing a god (identified by his horned head-dress) who holds out his right hand. Both wear plain robes and sit on either side of a date palm; behind them is a undulating serpent rising vertically." Readers familiar with the story of Adam and Eve in Genesis 2 - 3 will immediately perceive all the elements of the narrative on this seal – the central tree with fruit hanging from its branches, two anthropomorphic figures reaching for the fruit, and a snake. It comes as no surprise that early scholars from biblically literate cultures read the Adam and Eve narrative into this image. However, as is immediately apparent to contemporary scholars, this scene in its *Mesopotamian* context has little or no relationship to the *Israelite* scene in Genesis. The British Museum dates the image to either the third dynasty of Ur or the Akkadian period, approximately 2200 to 2100 BCE. The motif of a central tree with flanking figures is well attested during this time, is found over a broad geographic area, and the motif continues into the first millennium BCE.[5] Dominique Collon (1987:36), a widely known authority on cylinder seals, loosely relates this seal to the development of the banquet scene that includes two flanking figures with food or drink in the center. Interpreting the motif in light of scholarship on both iconography and ancient Near Eastern literature, Othmar Keel (1998:38) concludes that the scene of a central tree with flanking figures in its many manifestations is related to goddess and fertility cults. Interpreting the visual elements of a central tree, human figures, a serpent, mountains, and a figure suggestive of a cherubim found on a Syrian cylinder seal from the 18th-17th century BCE (see Figure Two), Keel suggests a possible Mesopotamian narrative counterpart to Genesis' use of the same visual features:

> "There the tree of life is simultaneously the tree of the world, supporting the constellations. A female deity, related to Ishtar by the eight-pointed star, holds her hand protectively over the tree. The chaos serpent, who was apparently about to attack the tree, is killed by Baal-Hadad, who strides over the mountains brandishing a mace. It is uncertain whether the griffin...is supposed to be the guardian of the tree of life..."(Keel 1997:51)

Figure One[6]

Figure Two[7]

There are echoes of Keel's hypothesized description among other scholars, relating the snake and tree to the goddess Asherah and the Asherah pole, for example.[8] Yet despite the similar constellation of images, the narrative of Genesis 2-3 still reads differently than scholars' attempts to explain non-Israelite uses of the same subjects. The most confident of associations between Genesis 3 and the goddess Asherah, for example, still must wrestle with the lack of textual referents in Genesis and the multiple hypotheses about what deities are actually present in Genesis' symbolism. It is common for such studies to note the literary sophistication of Genesis, using "universal symbols to tell a story that can be related across time and translated into the idiom of various cultures," therefore offering a literary explanation for why the author of Genesis 3 refrains from explicit references to Asherah, for example (Brown 2013:281). While that may be true, that a sophisticated author is undermining the Asherah cult in a very subtle yet powerful way, the present essay takes seriously a parallel or even alternative possibility – that the text betrays an author and/or original audience assumed to be familiar with the visual symbolism and some of its foreign use, but "illiterate" of its foreign indigenous meaning. Many biblical texts betray at least this much, that foreign cults existed in Israel, but the extent to which they were understood as indigenous to Israel's religious development is debated.

The first discussion at hand is the question of exposure: does Genesis 2-3 betray knowledge of the iconographic constellation of a central tree, flanking figures, and snake? Two textual clues suggest the answer is yes. The first and most obvious clue has already been implied: the spatial arrangement of the Garden narrative is the same as on the *Adam and Eve Seal*. There is at least one tree "in the middle" of the garden (Gen 2:9) and in the event that Eve eats the fruit, she gives some to her husband who was with her and he ate (Gen 3:6), indicating there are two figures next to the tree. Since the transgression happens immediately after Eve's discussion with the serpent, it is reasonable to deduce that the serpent is also near the central tree.[9] The second textual clue comes from scholarship's conversation regarding one of the more awkward textual elements of the Garden of Eden narrative, is there one or two trees? Interpreters of Genesis 2-3 have long been puzzled by the location and roles of the tree of knowledge and tree of life in Genesis 2-3. The tree of life enters the story in Genesis 2:9 as the first of two trees given names, "Out of the ground the LORD God made to grow every tree that is pleasant to the sight and good for food, the tree of life also in the midst of the garden, and the tree of the knowledge of good and evil" (NRSV). Without the greater context of Genesis 2-3, the most natural reading would be to assume that there are two trees and the tree of life is in the middle, with no explicit indication given about the location of the tree of knowledge. However, the conversation between the serpent and Eve indicates that the tree of knowledge is also in the middle of the garden (Gen 3:1-5). Considering the whole of Genesis 2-3, one must initially conclude that there are two trees in the middle of the garden, but this has not been unanimously accepted by interpreters of the text. Often cited is Eve's reference to the tree of knowledge as "*the* tree that is in the middle" (Gen 3:3), and the disappearance of any mention of the tree of life from 2:9-3:22. There is the sense that the sudden reappearance of the tree of life in 3:22, the only tree explicitly planted "in the middle," is confusing against the priority the tree of *knowledge* receives elsewhere in the narrative. These observations accentuate the awkward phrasing in 2:9 that makes the tree of knowledge look like an afterthought! Consequently, a number of commentators reading from a source critical perspective concluded that the tree of life has its roots in an older, independent narrative that was later incorporated with the present narrative that is about the tree of knowledge. Accordingly, they conclude, mentions of the tree of life in Genesis 3:22 and 24 are expansions not terribly relevant for the narrative as a whole, which is centered on the tree of knowledge.[10] LaCocque, rejecting source critical readings, has proposed one dual-natured tree at the center of the garden. In keeping with what he calls the "dialectical setting" of Genesis 2-3, he suggests that

> "J introduces here again a taut dialectic in his narrative. Departing from the mythical material at his disposal, he *splits* the tree into a tree of life and a tree of the knowledge of good and evil...Just as the Israelites were given through the law the choice between life and death, blessings and curses, Adam and Eve are presented with one tree with the potential for both life and death." (LaCocque 2006:47,69)

Regarding this question of one or two trees, the source critic's solution is to hypothesize two textual source traditions, while non-source critics speculate literary intentions for keeping the ambiguous description of the trees. Neither are satisfactory solutions to the presumed "problem" of one or two trees in the middle of the garden, but they *do* accentuate the observation being made here: that the Hebrew *text* as we have it is not clear about the number of trees.[11] I am suggesting that the evidence overlooked is visual. What if the narrative of Genesis 2-3 is a textual complement to what was already commonly known to the author or redactor and his audience through a *visual* medium? Returning to the motif on the *Adam and Eve Seal*, the central tree flanked by two figures is very prevalent in the catalogues of ancient Near Eastern seals known to us. The additional features of hanging fruit and a serpent are not commonly depicted together with the tree and figures in my own browsing of seal catalogues, but are common enough on cylinder seals in combination with one or more relevant subjects to hypothesize that those involved in producing the final text of Genesis 2-3 would have been exposed to a constellation of multiple subjects corresponding to the narrative. The central tree motif has been observed across a broad time period – from the Early Bronze through the Iron Age – and across all relevant geographic areas. Did the author literally have the *Adam and Eve Seal* available to him? Of course that is too speculative to defend, but exposure to the motif seems likely, especially when we consider the longevity of seals in both their original and stamped forms, their use in contexts that presume movement and cross-cultural contact, and even the number available to scholars thousands of years later (Gibson and Biggs 1977)!

A BIBLICAL INTERPRETATION OF THE ICONOGRAPHIC IMAGE

The iconographic approach to the garden narrative that I have offered here is conscious of the images potentially informing the author of Genesis 2-3. These images are not *secondary* to the available "mythical material" (I assume textual), from which the author diverges, as LaCocque suggested in his interpretation of Genesis 2-3. The best explanation for the textual "problem" of one or two trees in the garden may simply be the modern tendency to subordinate visual data. If one prioritizes visual data over textual, it is observed that the central tree motifs depicted on ancient cylinder seals have only one tree, and if visual data is among the *primary* material used by the author of Genesis 2-3, it is not surprising, therefore, that the text emphasizes one tree.[12] One could reasonably conclude that the biblical text is consciously associating a uniquely Israelite narrative with a visual medium that was familiar to him and his audience. This begs the question – then why two trees at all? Continuing with a method that prioritizes visual data, perhaps this is not a combination of multiple *textual* traditions about trees, but multiple *visual* traditions about trees. The single central tree is not the only scene known outside Israel. Although not as prevalent, some foreign scenes depict two trees in the center (Stager 2000:41). But significantly, iconographic studies of Jerusalem temple imagery suggest that Israel would have been familiar with the distinction of two trees among a garden of trees in sacred space. The two pillars in the temple vestibule were decorated with lilies, pomegranates, and other artistry implying trees (1 Kings 7:13-22). In addition to two tree-like columns towards the center of a temple complex, Psalm 92 describes transplanted trees in the surrounding sacred space, suggesting Eden's "trees of the garden." Pillars surrounded by temple or palace gardens are known at multiple ancient Near Eastern sacred sites.[13]

It has already been suggested that the Israelite conception of a central tree flanked by two figures as explained by the Adam and Eve story is unique versus its Mesopotamian visual parallel. One significant detour from Mesopotamian iconography is Genesis' depiction of human nature. Mesopotamian examples, including the *Adam and Eve Seal*, depict divine or royal figures at the center; some examples depict the god(dess) or king taking the place of the tree. This reflects a common theme in Near Eastern religious thought, that the king personifies the qualities of the tree, "the king himself represented the realization of [world] order in man, in other words, a true image of God, the Perfect Man" (Parpola 1993:168). Genesis 2-3 is similar in that it places the deity "among the trees of the garden" (Gen 3:8), but strikingly different in its description of humanity. Unlike Mesopotamian depictions of the universe that place a deity or king next to the tree, the story of *all humanity* in Genesis 2-3 unfolds next to the central tree(s). This would suggest that an Israelite anthropology grants a kind of "god-like" or "king-like" status to the *whole of humanity*, which is explicitly stated in Genesis 1.

The Eden narrative shows evidence of being exposed to a visual motif like the *Adam and Eve Seal*, yet significantly oblivious to the motif's native conceptual context. One might ask – *how* oblivious is the Fall narrative to the native conceptual context of the central tree motif? Because the story of the Fall differs noticeably from the cultic or mythic interpretations offered for the Mesopotamian tree with flanking figures, it seems difficult to postulate that the Adam and Eve narrative has much if any of the indigenous Mesopotamian myth, symbol, or cult in mind. Or, if it *is* understood (i.e. "iconographically *literate*"), the narrative must fall into the category of polemic, a text that is intentionally challenging a foreign worldview by providing an entirely alternative explanation for a visual constellation of figures. I find the former plausible – that the Eden narrative is in conversation with only the surface level visual elements of related cylinder seals, but significantly unaware of the details of its indigenous conceptual and mythic context. In Oswalt's terms, the visual similarities are "accidental," while the underlying differences are "essential." The Adam and Eve narrative may be *iconographically illiterate*, and despite its geographical and chronological proximity to Mesopotamian iconography, perhaps no more literate than its modern interpreter George Smith.

UNDERSTANDING VISUAL LITERACY

Because there is a plethora of studies that demonstrate significant cross cultural exposure of ancient Near Eastern texts and even iconography, it is reasonable to resist the suggestion being made here, that a text with geographic and chronological proximity to the culture that produced the central tree motif may be "illiterate" of its significance. Much like the conversations around iconographic method and biblical studies, there are many ways thinkers have approached the question of how visual data is produced and interpreted. Maria Avgerinou (2011:6-7), researching in the social scientific field of visual literacy, has incorporated the contributions of many scholars to arrive at a basic definition: Visual literacy is 1) "the learned ability to interpret visual messages accurately and to create such messages," and 2) "a group of largely acquired abilities, i.e., the abilities to understand (that is, read), and use (that is, write) images, as well as to think and learn in terms of images." Avgerinou continues by summarizing some of the foundational assertions that theorists in this field have in common. First, visual language ability develops prior to verbal ability. Second, visual language is learned. The meaning of a visual medium may be apparent on a basic level, but visual language is a complex code that must be learned for true comprehension. This predicts the third point, that visual literacy is culture specific. Fourth, research has shown that memory for pictures is superior to memory for words. This is called the "pictorial superiority effect." And lastly, texts and pictures are different languages that complement each other when they are used at the same time. This is called the "Dual coding memory model" - information presented in pictures is encoded twice, once as a picture, and once as a verbal label that names the picture. This creates a redundancy in the memory from which information can be retrieved either from the visual form or from the verbal memory (Augerinou 2011:7-13).

Can these observations of the human mind and human culture formation be applied to an ancient context? First, since the roots of biblical literature are either oral (textually illiterate), or produced in an ancient context that has a high illiterate population, one should expect visual communication to be very prevalent, if indeed visual language and visual memory are precursors to text production and textual memory. This resonates with current studies of biblical texts in light of iconographic evidence that emphasize that visual data is too often overlooked when reading biblical texts. I might add that not only is it too often overlooked, we likely underestimate how substantially primary visual data is for reconstructing ancient literary composition.

Second, visual literacy is a learned skill and culture specific. Images will acquire unique meanings in each culture that produces them. To be considered visually literate requires much more than a common use of the same subjects, or even a basic capacity to name subjects and their use in a scene. This suggests that neighboring cultures that demonstrate iconographic exchange at the surface can be dissimilar at a deeper conceptual level. Two contemporary observations would suggest that cultural proximity can be a misleading indicator of visual literacy. Consider first the Native American dream catcher that is often found hanging on non-native front porches, bedroom windows, and rearview mirrors. The dream catcher's most indigenous meaning is thought to have originated with the Ojibwe Nation, yet both non-native Americans and *native* non-Ojibwe nations use the symbol for reasons only superficially related to its indigenous mythic and ritual meaning (Oberholzer 1995:147).[14] A second example is the debate around the usefulness of "cultural literacy" exercises offered in American public schools.[15] In the area encompassing just one school district, students can be significantly uninformed about traditions they have been living alongside of for two hundred years or more. But returning to iconographic exchange between *ancient* cultures – this issue of geographic or chronological proximity as a predictor of cultural proximity has been discussed by Isaak de Hulster in his piece "Illuminating Images." Geographic and chronological proximity are often the primary considerations of iconographic borrowing. He advocates that iconographic studies should expand and consider cultural proximity, since two societies with geographic proximity may be significantly different in their culture and therefore the meaning they attach to images (de Hulster 2009:150-151).

On a related point, it seems important to distinguish proximity *within* the literature trade and exchanges between the discrete trades of literature and image production. One should consider the possibility that a *text* may be literate in the traditional literary sense because of shared scribal cultures, *and at the same time* visually illiterate if the scribe is not familiar with the production of cylinder seals, or the cultic culture that produces their motifs. Or to look at it from another perspective; whereas a Palestinian cylinder seal artist may be more literate with Mesopotamian motifs, a literary artist from the same geographic area interacting with visual material (like our author of Genesis 2-3 perhaps?) may not interpret it the same way or with the same underlying assumptions about its meaning. These points suggest that we should not be surprised if we encounter iconographically illiterate biblical texts. I have suggested the garden narrative of Genesis 2-3 as a possible candidate.

CONCLUSION

A related argument about Israelite religion was made in 1951 by Yehezkel Kaufmann, and proves relevant to the iconographic question at hand. He begins by noting that in the scholarly conversation regarding Israel's tolerance of foreign gods and foreign mythology, all perspectives agree, "throughout the Biblical period heathen mythology exercised a profound influence on Israelite culture" (Kaufmann 1951:179). This is argued primarily by comparing biblical data with non-Israelite religion as it is known from non-Israelite sources, paralleling one common method used in iconographic treatments of biblical texts. Kaufmann argues that "they have failed, however, to ask the primary question: what acquaintance do the Biblical writers *themselves* show with the nature of real non-Israelite religion, that is with mythological religion"? (Kaufmann 1951:179). I think this is similar to the question this essay seeks to answer– what level of visual literacy do the biblical writers *themselves* demonstrate regarding non-Israelite visual motifs, whether that be Egyptian, Syrian, or Mesopotamian? Is it possible that our contemporary access to the indigenous conceptual context of non-Israelite iconography may actually surpass that of the biblical writers? Kaufmann proceeds to make an argument that this may indeed be the case – that in his examination of biblical texts regarding idolatry, "the Bible shows absolutely no apprehension of the real character of mythological religion" (Kaufmann 1951:180). He compares a modern understanding of ancient polytheism, the underpinning of non-Israelite religion, with what the biblical text itself believes about the existence of "other gods." His conclusion is that for the biblical writers the realms of idolatry and myth are two separate spheres. Whereas in polytheism, the deification of nature gives birth to myth, which in turn deifies material objects – that is, the spheres of myth and idol worship are inextricably connected. Kaufmann argues that 1) the Bible never condemns belief in its own Yahwistic mythology even when it shares motifs with condemned non-Israelite religions, and 2) the Bible repeatedly condemns the practice of idolatry. Through a survey of biblical texts referencing idolatry, Kaufmann suggests that the biblical definition of idolatry is not the worship of living gods through lifeless idols, but simply what he calls a "fetishistic" worship of wood and stone (Kaufmann 1951:193). To put it in terms of the present essay, Kaufmann suggests that the biblical texts regarding idolatry demonstrate illiteracy of foreign myth.

John Oswalt (2009:12-13) reminds us that the evidence available to Kaufmann in his time is not substantially different than what is available to twenty-first century scholars. Consequently, both Kaufmann's and Oswalt's ideas are timely contributions to contemporary inquiries about the origins of Israelite religion. The present interpretation of Genesis 2-3 in its iconographic context is, in the spirit of John Oswalt's *Bible Among the Myths*, offered as a contribution to the ongoing discussion of Israel's religious origins and unique worldview.

End Notes

[1] For an in depth treatment see Oswalt, *The Bible Among the Myths*, 47-84 where he explains the Israelite worldview as "transcendence," versus the ancient Near Eastern worldview as "continuity." He applies this argument to the prophetic corpus in John Oswalt, "Is There Anything Unique in the Israelite Prophets?" *BSac* 172 (2015): 67-84.

[2] The word "iconography" is a very broad term, often used for the study of symbol in all genres of art. Here, I am referring to the interpretation of ancient Near Eastern visual material. For the theoretical foundations of this method, two excellent starting points are Izaak de Hulster, "Illuminating Images: A Historical Position and Method for Iconographic Exegesis," in *Iconography and Biblical Studies* (AOAT 361: Munster: Ugarit-Verlag, 2009), 139-62 and Joel LeMon, "Iconographic Approaches: The Iconic Structure of Psalm 17," in *Method Matters: Essays on the Interpretation of the Hebrew Bible in Honor of David L. Petersen* (ed. J. LeMon and K. H. Richards; Atlanta: SBL, 2009), 143-68. See also several dictionary entries: M. Klingbeil, "Psalm 5: Iconography," in *Dictionary of the Old Testament: Wisdom, Poetry & Writings* (ed. by T. Longman III and P. Enns; Downers Grove: IVP, 2008), 621-31 and Brent Strawn, "Imagery," in *Dictionary of the Old Testament: Wisdom, Poetry & Writings* (ed. by T. Longman III and P. Enns; Downers Grove: IVP, 2008). Also Christina Bosserman, "Iconography" in *The Lexham Bible Dictionary*.

[3] Joel LeMon references several such studies in his discussion of three "typologies" of iconographic study in LeMon, "Iconographic Approaches," 146-52.

[4] See also T. Mitchell, *The Bible in the British Museum: Interpreting the Evidence* (London: The British Museum Press, 2004), 24.

[5] This can be observed by browsing well-documented seal and iconography collections. Four good sources for tree imagery are Othmar Keel and C. Uehlinger, *Gods, Goddesses, and Images of God* (trans. T. H. Trapp; Minneapolis: Fortress, 1998), Othmar Keel, *The Symbolism of the Biblical World: Ancient Near Eastern Iconography and the Book of Psalms* (trans. T. Hallett; Winona Lake: Eisenbrauns, 1997), Dominique Collon, *First Impressions: Cylinder Seals in the Ancient Near East* (London: British Museum Press, 2005), and Othmar Keel, *Goddesses and Trees,*

New Moon and Yahweh: Ancient Near Eastern Art and the Hebrew Bible. (JSOTSup 261; Sheffield: Sheffield Academic Press, 1998).

[6] Permission to use for non-commercial purposes, British Museum. http://www.britishmuseum.org/research/ collection_online/collection_object _details.aspx?objectId=368842&partId=1&searchText=adam+and+eve+seal& page=1.

[7] Public Domain. http://www.metmuseum.org/art/collection/search/327185?sortBy=Relevance &deptids=3&ft=cylinder+seal+moore&offset=60&rpp= 20&pos=76.

[8] For an extended review of the scholarship around Asherah and Genesis 3, see Joel Brown, "The Goddess and the Garden: The Israelite Understanding of the Genesis 3 Narrative" (Ph.D. diss; The Graduate Theological Union, 2013).

[9] A variant of Genesis 3:3 reads "But from the fruit of *this* tree which is in the middle of the garden" lending support to the proposed scene that puts all the characters – man, woman, and serpent – next to the tree.

[10] C. Westermann, *Genesis 1-11: A Commentary* (Minneapolis: Augsburg, 1984), 211, 271. Westermann references Stade, Budde, and Gunkel's analagous source critical interpretations. A more recent example is David Carr. "The Politics of Textual Subversion: A Diachronic Perspective on the Garden of Eden Story." *JBL* 112 (1993): 577-95.

[11] Among other creative solutions is Paul Humbert, *Etudes sur le récit du paradis et de la chute dans la Genèse* (Neuchatel: Secrétariat de l'Université, 1940), 22-3 where he hypothesizes that the tree of life is hidden to Adam and Eve, so in 2:9, the tree of life is not pertinent information. Comparing the life-giving plant, food, and water in the Gilgamesh Epic and Adapa myth with the tree of life in Genesis, he concludes that like these substances the tree of life was hidden.

[12] A plant that magically bestows immortality is known from the Epic of Gilgamesh, and it may be argued that the absence of multiple magic plants or trees

in Mesopotamian texts would be evidence for the same conclusion, that Genesis is merely accommodating its narrative to a context that speaks of a single magic plant. However, the visual medium in this case is far more compelling as a "source" for Genesis' tree of life than the Epic of Gilgamesh that lacks other features of the visual motif, such as the central location of the tree and its association with dual figures (and/or a serpent, mountain, rivers, and cherubim!).

[13] For a more thorough study of temple architecture and iconography as depicting an earthly Eden, see Lawrence Stager, "Jerusalem and the Garden of Eden," *Eretz-Israel: Archaeological, Historical, and Geographical Studies* 26 (1999): 183-94.

[14] See also Philip Jenkins, *Dream Catchers: How Mainstream America Discovered Native Spirituality*. New York: Oxford University Press, 2004.

[15] The debate can be observed in two ideologically opposed articles: Bernard Schweizer, "Cultural Literacy: Is it Time to Revisit the Debate?" *Thought and Action* 25 (2009): 51-56 and Leila Christenbury, "Cultural literacy: A Terrible Idea Whose Time Has Come," *The English Journal* 78 (1989): 14-17.

WORKS CITED

Avgerinou, Maria D.
    2011   "Toward a Cohesive Theory of Visual Literacy." *Journal of
            Visual Literacy* 30: 1-19.

Bosserman, Christina
    2012-15 "Iconography," In *The Lexham Bible Dictionary*. Edited
            by D. Barry, D. Bomar, D. R. Brown, R. Klippenstein,
            D. Mangum, C. Sinclair Wolcott, É W. Widder.
            Bellingham, WA: Lexham Press.

Brown, Joel
    2013   "The Goddess and the Garden: The Israelite Understanding
            of the Genesis 3 Narrative." Ph.D. diss., The Graduate
            Theological Union.

Carr, David
    1993   "The Politics of Textual Subversion: A Diachronic Perspective
            on the Garden of Eden Story." *Journal of Biblical Literature*
            112: 577-95.

Christenbury, Leila
    1989   "Cultural literacy: A Terrible Idea Whose Time Has Come."
            The English Journal 78: 14-17.

Collon, Dominique
    2005   *First Impressions: Cylinder Seals in the Ancient Near East.*
            London: British Museum Press.

de Hulster, Izaak
    2009   "Illuminating Images: A Historical Position and Method
            for Iconographic Exegesis," Pages 139-62 in *Iconography
            and Biblical Studies*. Alter Orient und Altes Testament 361.
            Munster: Ugarit-Verlag.

Gibson, McGuire and R. D. Biggs, eds.
  1977   *Seals and Sealing in the Ancient Near East.* Bibliotheca mesopotamica 6. Malibu: Udena Publications.

Humbert, Paul
  1940   *Etudes sur le récit du paradis et de la chute dans la Genèse.* Neuchatel: Secrétariat de l'Université.

Jenkins, Philip
  2004   *Dream Catchers: How Mainstream America Discovered Native Spirituality.* New York: Oxford University Press.

Kaufmann, Yehezkel
  1951   "The Bible and Mythological Polytheism," *Journal of Biblical Literature* 70: 179-97.

Keel, Othmar and C. Uehlinger
  1998   *Gods, Goddesses, and Images of God.* Trans. T. H. Trapp. Minneapolis: Fortress.

  1998   *Goddesses and Trees, New Moon and Yahweh: Ancient Near Eastern Art and the Hebrew Bible.* Journal for the Study of the Old Testament SupplementSeries 261. Sheffield: Sheffield Academic Press.

  1997   *The Symbolism of the Biblical World: Ancient Near Eastern Iconography and the Book of Psalms.* Trans. T. Hallett. Winona Lake: Eisenbrauns.

Klingbeil, Martin
  2008   "Psalm 5: Iconography," Pages 621-31 in *Dictionary of the Old Testament: Wisdom, Poetry & Writings.* Edited by T. Longman III and P. Enns. Downers Grove: IVP.

LaCocque, Andre
  2006   *The Trial of Innocence: Adam, Eve, and the Yahwist.* Eugene, OR: Cascade.

LeMon, Joel
2009   "Iconographic Approaches: The Iconic Structure of Psalm 17,"
        Pages 143-68 in *Method Matters: Essays on the Interpretation
        of the Hebrew Bible in Honor of David L. Petersen.* Edited by J.
        LeMon and K.H. Richards. Atlanta: SBL.

Mitchell, T.
2004   *The Bible in the British Museum: Interpreting the Evidence.*
        London: The British Museum Press.

Oberholzer, Cath
1995   "The Re-Invention of Tradition and the Marketing of
        Cultural Values." *Anthropologica* 37: 141-53.

Oswalt, John
2015   "Is There Anything Unique in the Israelite Prophets?"
        Bibliotheca Sacra 172: 67-84.

2009   *The Bible Among the Myths.* Grand Rapids: Zondervan.

Parpola, S.
1993   "The Assyrian Tree of Life: Tracing the Origins of Jewish
        Monotheism and Greek Philosophy," *Journal of Near Eastern
        Studies* 52: 161-208.

Schweizer, Bernard
2009   "Cultural Literacy: Is it Time to Revisit the Debate?" *Thought
        and Action* 25: 51-56.

Smith, George
1876   *The Chaldean Account of Genesis.* London: Sampson Low,
        Marion, Searle & Rivington.

Stager, Lawrence E.
2000   "Jerusalem as Eden," *Biblical Archaeology Review* 26:41.

1999   "Jerusalem and the Garden of Eden," *Eretz-Israel:
        Archaeological, Historical, and Geographical Studies* 26: 183-94.

Strawn, Brent
    2008   "Imagery," Pages 306-314 in *Dictionary of the Old Testament: Wisdom, Poetry & Writings*. Edited by T. Longman III and P. Enns. Downers Grove: IVP.

Westermann, C.
    1984   *Genesis 1-11: A Commentary*. Minneapolis: Augsburg.

Paganism, Wesley, and the Means of Grace[1]

JOSEPH R. DONGELL

KEYWORDS:

John Wesley, Methodism, love, paganism, Means of Grace

Joseph R. Dongell (PhD, Union Theological Seminary) is a Professor of Biblical Studies at Asbury Theological Seminary in Wilmore, Kentucky.

ABSTRACT

John Wesley, the 18th century English reformer and father of Methodism, can be read with justification as the leader of a Christian renewal movement whose deepest underpinnings lay squarely in the Old Testament. I will identify three primary anchorages, describing the first two briefly before treating the third more extensively. To put it succinctly, I claim that Wesley cast the *goal* of his vision as the love commanded for God and neighbor in Deut. 6:4-5 and Lev. 19:18, identified the *content* of that love in terms of the Mosaic Law itself, then urged the *attainment* of such love through practicing the Means of Grace in a manner congruent with the theology of Malachi 3:6-12.

Introduction

John Wesley, the 18th century English reformer and father of Methodism, can be read with justification as the leader of a Christian renewal movement whose deepest underpinnings lay squarely in the Old Testament. I will identify three primary anchorages, describing the first two briefly before treating the third more extensively. To put it succinctly, I claim that Wesley cast the *goal* of his vision as the love commanded for God and neighbor in Deut. 6:4-5 and Lev. 19:18, identified the *content* of that love in terms of the Mosaic Law itself, then urged the *attainment* of such love through practicing the Means of Grace in a manner congruent with the theology of Malachi 3:6-12.

The Goal: Love

Wesley never tired of citing Deuteronomy and Leviticus when describing the character to which Methodists must aspire: "Who is a Methodist? A Methodist is… one who "loves the Lord his God with all his heart, and with all his soul, and with all his mind, and with all his strength."[2] Or again, "Religion we conceive to be no [thing] other than love; the love of God and of all mankind; the loving God 'with all our heart, and soul, and strength,' and the loving of every soul which God hath made, every man on earth as our own soul."[3]

When alluding to these passages (Deut. 6:5, Lev. 19:18), Wesley never supposed they originated *de novo* from the lips of Jesus, as if love suddenly appeared in the first century CE as a uniquely Christian ethic. Instead, Wesley grounded love's priority in its longitudinal distribution across the whole work of God: "Love is the end [i.e. goal], the sole end, of every dispensation of God, from the beginning of the world to the consummation of all things."[4]

More precisely with regard to the Old Testament, Wesley named Moses as the first voice in the lineage of those proclaiming love: "[This religion of love] is the religion of the Bible, as no one can deny who reads it with any attention. It is the religion which is continually inculcated therein, which runs through both the Old and New Testament. Moses and the prophets, our blessed Lord and his Apostles, proclaim with one voice, 'Thou shalt love the Lord thy God with all thy soul, and thy neighbour as thyself."[5] A good Methodist, in Wesley's view, would self-consciously advocate for that religion of love required by God already in the Bible's earliest collection of books, the Pentateuch.

THE CONTENT OF LOVE: THE LAW

Protestantism cannot be thought of apart from the person and message of Martin Luther. To our minds come the 95 theses he nailed to the church door at Wittenburg, his blustery battles with Catholic authorities, and the three "*sola's*" that capture the essence of the Reformation. Ask a seminarian to name the core of Luther's crusade, and you'll likely hear an adaptation from the wording of Romans and Galatians, like "…salvation by grace, through faith, apart from the law…"

One of Wesley's encounters with Luther's legacy is well known. In his journal throughout May of 1738 Wesley portrayed himself as a spiritually distressed, but fervently seeking soul. This was but the nadir of 10 years of tortuous descent that included a failed missionary venture to Georgia and a terrifying brush with death during a ferocious storm at sea. But as all Methodists know, a breakthrough would come in London on May 24. In Wesley's words, "In the evening I went very unwillingly to a society in Aldersgate Street, where someone was reading Luther's preface to the Epistle to the Romans. About a quarter before nine, while he was describing the change, which God works in the heart through faith in Christ, I felt my heart strangely warmed. I felt I did trust Christ, Christ alone for salvation: And an assurance was given to me, that he had taken away *my* sins, even *mine*, and saved *me* from the law of sin and death."[6]

Given only this part of the story, one can be forgiven for imagining that a simple, straight line runs from Luther right through Wesley, as if Wesleyan theology should identify itself without nuance as "Protestant," and should build upon Luther's formulations without modification. But three years later (June 15, 1741) in the same journal we read of another encounter with Luther's works, yielding a more studied assessment:

> I set out for London, and read over in the way, that celebrated book, Martin Luther's "Commentary on the Epistle to the Galatians." I was utterly ashamed. How have I esteemed this book, only because I heard it so commended by others; or, at best, because I had read some excellent sentences occasionally quoted from it!

But what shall I say, now that I judge for myself?. . . . [H]ow blasphemously does he speak of good works and the Law of God; constantly coupling the Law with sin, death, hell, or the devil; and teaching, that Christ delivers us from them all alike. Whereas it can no more be proved by Scripture that Christ delivers us from the Law of God, than that he delivers us from holiness or from heaven. Here (I apprehend) is the real spring of the grand error of the Moravians. They follow Luther, for better for worse. Hence their "No works; no Law; no commandments."[7]

Filled with remorse for having endorsed Luther's work on Galatians before reading it, Wesley determined the next day to mend the matter. "I thought it my bounden duty openly to warn the congregation against that dangerous treatise; and to retract whatever recommendation I might ignorantly have given of it."[8]

Even if we grant that Wesley had not adequately grasped Luther's whole thought about the Law, we should not be surprised that Luther's rhetoric (which is quite susceptible to being read as antinomian) provoked such a strong rebuke from Wesley. The father of Methodism had been waging a fierce battle against antinomian voices both inside and outside the Methodist movement. At least three of the 52 Standard Sermons directly address the role of the Law in the Christian life, leaving no room for doubt in the mind of the reader. As Wesley saw it, the Mosaic Law was comprised of two streams of content: the ceremonial and the moral. Regarding the ceremonial law, Wesley quite agreed, "our Lord did come to destroy, to dissolve, and utterly abolish [it]." But regarding the moral law, Wesley insisted that Christ "did not take [it] away."[9] Furthermore,

It was not the design of [Jesus'] coming to revoke any part of [the moral law]. This is a law which never can be broken, which "stands fast as the faithful witness in heaven."... Every part of this law must remain in force upon all mankind, and in all ages; as not depending either on time or place, or any other circumstances liable to change, but on the nature of God, and the nature of man, and their unchangeable relation to each other.[10]

What should be clear, now, is that the *content* of Wesley's "religion of love" was not to be filled by subjective moral reflection, but by the moral vision revealed specifically and authoritatively in the Law of Moses. The gospel of grace with its ethic of love "continually leads us to a *more exact fulfilling of the law*" (emphasis added).[11]

The Attainment of Love: The Means of Grace

But even if these two points are granted, a crucial third issue remains: *How* does one enter into such a life of love? *How* does one become a person who actually loves God and neighbor, a person whose very character, disposition, and affections are ruled by love?

For most contemporary Arminians the answer is clear: "Just do it! Just decide now to act in loving ways toward everyone!" But such "decisionism" betrays, under biblical and theological analysis, both an overestimation of human willpower and an underestimation of the selfishness in the human heart, even the redeemed human heart. Pure universal love cannot be generated from within, even by our best intentions and highest energies.

Wesley astutely recognized that love has its origin ultimately in God (I John 4:7), and that any profusion of love *from* the human heart (toward God and others) depends directly upon a prior infusion of love from God *into* one's heart. As Wesley put it in a particularly trenchant passage in *A Plain Account of Christian Perfection*:

> [One cause of] a thousand mistakes is [this:]... not considering deeply enough that love is the highest *gift* of God; humble, gentle, patient love; that all visions, revelations, [or] manifestations whatever, are little things compared to love; and that all [other] *gifts* ... are either the same with or infinitely inferior to [love].[12] (emphasis added)

Once we recognize the *gift*-nature of love, we can refine the question at hand, asking now how to *receive from God* the necessary infusion of love. Put more generally, is there anything we can "do" to obtain from God the "benefits" we are seeking? Can human action precipitate divine grace?

A Question of Means

This question has been, in real sense, the perennial religious question facing humanity throughout the millennia, not to mention across the pages of scripture. It touches on nothing less than the nature of the divine-human interaction, requiring the practitioners of all religions to create or embrace a worldview accounting for all reality: the divine, the human, and material worlds. The nature of the worldview one adopts will determine the nature of the practices deployed for obtaining "divine benefits."

Wesley faced this same question in his own day. On the one hand, those fervently seeking an intense relationship with God perceived that most Church of England attendees had slipped into a lazy and lifeless ritualism. As long as they participated in rites of the Church, they imagined, all would be well with their souls. Such matters as faith and obedience had been bracketed out, it seemed, as irrelevant.

Wanting no part of the deadness of the established church, many within the revival movement were of a mind to cast off every vestige of the old. Some were recommending that seekers retreat into a radically passive faith of laying aside all religious rites and practices. No prayer, no reading of scripture, no participation in the Lord's Supper should pollute a naked faith in Christ with "works."[13]

The advocates of passivity could appeal not only to the rhetoric from the Continental Reformation (e.g. *sola fide*), but to an assortment of OT passages. Throughout the prophets and Psalms can be found declarations that God "has no delight in sacrifice," or that God "would not be pleased" should a burnt offering be offered.[14] To the same point, they apparently quoted God's instructions to Israel as they stood on the brink of extinction at the hands of the Egyptian army: "Fear not, stand firm, and see the salvation of the Lord, which he will work for you today... The Lord will fight for you, and you have only to be still" (Ex. 14:13-14).[15]

Wesley stood on the horns of a dilemma. On the one hand, he could join the Quietists in dismissing human action altogether and embrace divine monergism. One could imagine that this move might protect certain understandings of grace, faith, and divine sovereignty all at once. The opposite option would be for Wesley to assert the efficacy of human effort/action in obtaining divine favor, and to reimpose religious practices, that, in the perception of many, had so crippled the true gospel with an insipid humanism.

But Wesley chose neither pathway, charting a course he judged to be the Bible's true teaching as recognized by faithful Christians all along. In his sermon "The

Means of Grace," he laid out a vision that valued human action as the condition for receiving God's gifts, without attributing merit or effectiveness to them.[16]

For this sermon's subtitle Wesley chose Malachi 3:7, "Ye are gone away from mine ordinances, and have not kept them." And though Wesley did not exegete this passage in this sermon, his arguments within the sermon correspond closely to the Malachi's claims and implicit theology. Put another way, Wesley's articulation of a theology of the Means of Grace is indebted to the Old Testament's articulation of appropriate human-divine interaction as biblical writers battled the ever-present lure of paganism. But what was paganism? Why was it so alluring? And how does this relate to the Means of Grace?

THE NATURE OF PAGANISM[17]

With good reason contemporary pagans claim that paganism is mankind's natural outlook on reality, standing as "the ancestral religion of the whole of humanity."[18] It was no isolated ancient phenomenon limited to Israel's neighbors, or to the polytheistic excesses of Greco-Roman civilization. Nor should paganism be thought of as backwards, primitive, or easily dislodged by modernity. In truth, paganism has maintained a tenacious hold on humanity throughout the ages,[19] being espoused by social and intellectual elites even in Christian societies, always creeping into the camps of its primary opponents: classical Judaism, historic Christianity, and Islam.

Its basic characteristics are remarkably stable, in spite of its diverse manifestations across the millennia. In an illuminating book edited by two English neo-Pagans, such contemporary Northern European streams as Heathenism, Druidry, Wicca, Left-Hand Ritual Magick, Shamanism, Sacred Ecology, and Darklight Philosophy are gathered together and treated as flowing from the common fountainhead of ancient (pre-Christian) paganism. And though one leading proponent insists on referring to the plurality of pagan "theologies," she does not shrink from identifying the planks shared by nearly all forms of paganism, whether ancient, medieval, or modern.[20]

At paganism's core is the conviction that all things (the divine, gods, goddesses, humanity, all natural phenomena, and time itself) are woven together into a one-ness, a singularity, into the "world-all." There is a fundamental *ontological continuity* between all things, such that all things form one organic, permanently interconnected whole.[21] To borrow images from the modern world, we may say that everything is "hardwired together," or that every part of reality is "connected to the cosmic web."

Because no clean distinctions can be made between the various elements of reality, two seemingly contradictory claims are simultaneously true within the pagan worldview. On the one hand, since divine energy saturates all things in their plurality, pagans advocate polytheism. And given the fluidity of all boundaries, divine-human interaction can take place with relative ease, especially as human beings discern the intimate connections pulsing between themselves and all other powers.[22] As a shaman might express it, "The Otherworld is this world—there are no barriers. It burns through me with a passion and a delight. The life of the earth is sacred, and is a part of the Infinite."[23]

This thoroughgoing interpenetration between the divine, the human, and natural worlds implies an intimacy between these realms grounded *simply in their being*. Since all the forces of nature (including the human body) are alive with divine energy, it is inevitable that the earth itself be reverenced as the goddess from whom our vitality flows, in much the same way as the human fetus (and newborn) draws its life-fluid and sustenance from its biological mother. This explains the strong pagan predilection toward worshiping nature and elevating the feminine.[24]

On the other hand, the multiplicity of gods and goddesses naturally implies a meta-divine, that singular divine power beyond the multiplicity unifying all things into the "world-all."[25] In this regard, pagans speak of the Source, or the Oneness, or the Power operative behind all things. But because personhood requires a certain maintenance of boundaries between oneself and all that is "other," it is immediately understandable why the ultimate Oneness of pagan imagination will be non-personal.[26]

If at paganism's core is an *ontological* continuity between all things, the pagan naturally presumes an *epistemological* continuity between all things. After all, if everything is hardwired together, then anyone with sufficient determination should be able to "hack" into any "site" in the "web" of the universe to learn of future events or explore divine mysteries. In principle, no secrets can be hidden from the (human) practitioner who masters pagan arts of divination. Nature, understood all inclusively, is "rich in potential revelations of all kinds, and must be read as one reads a book."[27] Accordingly, the notion of divine-revelation-from-the-outside is repugnant to pagans who, by virtue of their worldview, sense no need of help in navigating throughout the all-inclusive Oneness of which they are already an intimate part.

If the pagan can (in principle) *understand* all hidden mysteries of divine power, then the next step is to *use* that knowledge to bring about desired effects in the tangible world. In other words, *epistemological* continuity leads to *causative* continuity. Accordingly, Faivre defines magic as "at once the *knowledge* of the network of sympathies or antipathies which bind the things of Nature and the concrete *implementation* of this knowledge."[28] Similarly, Prudence Jones describes magic as "an active wielding of the hidden powers," exercised "by manipulating the invisible, intangible world."[29] Here we see the importance of ritual and rite. If the practitioner has *rightly understood* the hidden connections at work, and has then *rightly performed* a ritual, then the desired effect *must come to pass*. Ironically, paganism subscribes as firmly to a cause-effect universe as does the modern scientific world.

But if pagans envision themselves as bringing hidden forces to bear on the affairs of human life, the question of ethics immediately surfaces. Is one kind of magic "black," and another "white"? Can magic be used in immoral ways?

On its website the Pagan Federation International espouses an ethic of "do no harm," and forbids magic to be deployed "for unfair personal gain."[30] But these phrases find no elaboration in an otherwise expansive presentation of paganism, and are conspicuous for their terseness. It may be that this rather light brushing on the question of morality stems from the nature of paganism itself, for which, as pagan advocate Prudence Jones puts it, "there is no absolute evil."[31]

And this would seem the necessary outcome of the initial premise of paganism as proposed above: that all reality intermingles into a great oneness where no clean distinctions can be made. If all things inseparably interpenetrate one another, then even an ultimate distinction between good and evil cannot be sustained. And yet precisely this loss draws Darklight Philosophy advocate Shan Jayran to prefer paganism to any religious system [e.g. Christianity] espousing a "dualistic" outlook, that is, an outlook maintaining a fundamental distinction between good and evil. As he explains:

> What is not open to a dualistic theology [as it is to paganism] is to relinquish the all-good God... We [pagans] can return to a

wholeness neither good nor evil, but natural. The 'Force' or 'Source'
is not good or evil, just utterly complete.[32]

If it is true that paganism tends to move beyond the fundamental distinction
between good and evil, it is also true that the effectiveness of pagan ritual does
not depend upon the morality of the practitioner. For if rites are grounded solely
in an accurate knowledge of hidden power and in their precise performance, then
those rites should unfailingly produce the desired effects, apart from the ethical
character of the participants. In other words, *moral* continuity and the collapse
of a fundamental distinction between good and evil guarantees that the *causative*
continuity allowing the manipulation of cosmic powers will not be interrupted by
moral constraints.

THE NATURE OF YAHWISM

In turning now to the biblical worldview, we acknowledge that Israelite
religious practices must have appeared similar to those of their pagan neighbors.
But we should not imagine that such similarities prove that Israel shared in their
pagan worldview. In being called from Ur, Abraham was being separated from his
kinsmen not only geographically, but theologically as well.

The God who revealed himself to Abraham would, in time, make it clear that
he was *ontologically dis-continuous* with the cosmos. Human beings are not bits
and pieces of the divine being, and have not sprung up from blood, or sweat, or
semen of gods and goddesses.[33] Though the world is fully open to YHWH acting
within and upon it, YHWH remains "wholly other" from it. There is no ladder of
progression between the two.[34]

Such ontological dis-continuity leads to *epistemological* dis-continuity: human
beings cannot probe the mind of God, or unravel divine secrets. We are, instead,
radically dependent upon God's gracious choice of self-revelation. It is from outside
ourselves and the cosmos that we learn (from God) about God's character, about
God's plans for the cosmos, and about God's particular will for his people.[35]

Furthermore, the God of Abraham would make it clear that no ritual would
trap him or force his hand. Not even would *rightly performed rituals that God
himself had revealed and commanded* compel God to act. In other words, there was

causative dis-continuity between the rites performed by Israelites and the outcomes they desired.

Having emphatically revealed himself as holy, as *morally dis-continuous* with and untainted by evil, Israel's God mandated that she likewise manifest the same clear and clean separation from all evil: "Be ye holy, for I am holy."[36]

WESLEY AND MALACHI 3

I contend that most of these elements distinguishing Yahwism from paganism are expressed or implied in Malachi 3, the passage Wesley invoked when articulating a biblical theology of the Means of Grace. Throughout Malachi's striking question-answer encounter between YHWH and his wayward people, there is no hint of a meta-divine, of powers above or beyond YHWH to which Israel might appeal. YHWH himself is the only God of record, the One who has created all things (2:10, 15), and whose name is great among all the nations (1:11, 14). This God *stands distinct from and in full control of nature*: on his own terms he can open the windows of heaven and pour down refreshing rains (3:10), suppress ruinous pests, and cause crops to flourish (3:11).

Given such ontological discontinuity, Israel must then depend upon God's self-revelation (and not upon sorcerers, 3:5) for knowing how to please YHWH and receive his blessing (*epistemological discontinuity*). The "how" of returning to God will consist simply in obeying the instructions already revealed at Sinai: "Remember the law of my servant Moses, the statutes and ordinances that I commanded him at Horeb for all Israel" (4:4, cf. 3:7). From Wesley's perspective as well, the (instituted) Means of Grace are not strategies *we invent or intuit* for incurring God's favor.[37] These Means, it is crucial to note, are *given to us* in scripture *by God himself*. If we desire to receive blessings from God, we must seek them *in the pathways that are themselves God's gifts to us!* [38]

But it is apparent in Malachi that Israel had discovered that her sacrificial rites had become ineffective (*causal discontinuity*). The prophet declared, "You cover the Lord's altar with tears, with tears and weeping and groaning because he no longer regards the offering or accepts it with favor at your hand." It seems they were staring at dry fields and withered crops (implied by 3:10-11), somehow unable to coerce divine blessing despite their fervent cultic worship. They were discovering what Wesley would emphatically teach his followers: "Before you use any means, let it be deeply impressed on your soul, -- there is no *power* in this. It is, in itself, a poor, dead empty thing: Separate from God, it is a dry leaf, a shadow."[39]

But what was Israel's underlying problem? She had flouted God's holy standards. Many had scuttled their marriages, ignoring the solemn covenant made with their wives (2:14-16). Others swore falsely, or had oppressed the hireling in wages, or had oppressed widow and orphan, or had thrust out sojourners (3:5). As the entire book of Malachi implies, Israel must return to God in heartfelt repentance that must involve an across-the-board embrace of God's law and a mirroring of God's character. Apart from a moral realignment and an eschewing of evil, Israel's cultic worship would have no effect. Holiness cannot abide unholiness: *moral discontinuity*.

So too did Wesley insist that the Means of Grace be employed specifically within an ethical framework, for "the renewal of our soul in righteousness and true holiness."[40] And as we await the full renewal in the (moral) image of God, Wesley believed that the only acceptable mode of living was one of "universal obedience in a zealous keeping of all the commandments."[41] This tight connection forged between ethics and practicing the Means of Grace stands light years removed from the moral disinterestedness of standard paganism as it seeks to access hidden powers.

Finally, we note that at the climax of his sermon Wesley reminds his readers to "seek God alone... Nothing but God can satisfy your soul."[42] Such a soul-satisfying God cannot be an impersonal force, an abstract power of utter completeness. So too the God of Malachi is unmistakably personal: a God who speaks, loves, warns, argues, promises, curses, and urges towards the kind of repentance that will lead Israel into obedient trust, into a restored personal relationship with himself.[43]

In short, we can discern Wesley's profound debt to the Old Testament in terms of three critical issues defining his movement. As he saw them, Methodists were those seeking to be transformed into persons who loved God and neighbor (Deut. 6:4-5; Lev. 19:18), who understood the content of that love as initially revealed within the Law of Moses, and who sought this transformation by walking in the divinely instituted means of grace according to the theological vision exemplified in Malachi.

END NOTES

[1] I gladly join the other writers in this volume in celebrating the ministry of John Oswalt: anointed preacher, master teacher, incisive scholar, and friend. John has tirelessly and effectively served the Church and her Lord in countless venues, all to the glory of God.

[2] John Wesley, "The Character of a Methodist," in *The Works of John Wesley*, Thomas Jackson ed., 3rd Edition (London: Wesleyan Conference Office, 1872), VIII: 341.

[3] Wesley, "Principles of a Methodist Farther Explained," VIII: 474.

[4] Wesley, "The Law Established Through Faith" (sermon XXXVI) V: 462.

[5] Wesley, "On Laying the Foundation of the New Chapel, Near the City-Road, London" (sermon CXXXII) VII: 424.

[6] Wesley, Journal entry for May 24, 1738, I: 103.

[7] Wesley, Journal entry for June 15, 1741, I: 315-16.

[8] Wesley, Journal entry for June 16, 1741, I: 316.

[9] Wesley, "Upon Our Lord's Sermon on the Mount, Discourse V" (sermon XXV) V: 311.

[10] Wesley, "Upon Our Lord's Sermon on the Mount, Discourse V" (sermon XXV) V: 311.

[11] Wesley, "Upon Our Lord's Sermon on the Mount, Discourse V" (sermon XXV) V: 313-14.

[12] Wesley, "A Plain Account of Christian Perfection," XI: 430.

[13] This is evident in Wesley's direct reference to Exodus 14, and his rebuttal of their interpretation of it by appealing to the immediately following context. Wesley, "The Means of Grace," (sermon XVI) V: 197.

[14] These citations are from Psalm 51:16. Compare with Psalm 51:7-15.

[15] Wesley, "The Means of Grace" (sermon XVI) V: 197. Quote from sermon on Means of Grace about Exodus 14.

[16] Wesley, "The Means of Grace" (sermon XVI) V: 200. We may view Wesley as avoiding two opposite errors: that of overvaluing the Means of Grace, and that of undervaluing them. On this see Kenneth J. Collins and Jason E. Vickers, eds. The Sermons of John Wesley: A Collection for the Christian Journey (Nashville: Abingdon, 2013) p. 70.

[17] I depend significantly upon Oswalt's analysis of paganism and Yahwism, but seek to support his claims about paganism by citing modern pagan writers who embrace paganism as a continuous tradition (in its essence) from the earliest human religious instincts to the present. For Oswalt's analysis, see his *The Bible among the Myths: Unique Revelation or Just Ancient Literature?* (Grand Rapids, MI: Zondervan, 2009), pp. 47-62 (of paganism), and pp. 63-84 (of Yahwism).

[18] Under the sub-heading of "What is Paganism" on the website of The Pagan Federation. www.paganfederation.org.

[19] Ronald Hutton lays out a number of pagan trajectories across the centuries, in "The Roots of Modern Paganism," *Paganism Today: Wiccans, Druids, the Goddess and Ancient Earth Traditions for the Twenty-First Century*, Graham Harvey and Charlotte Hardman, eds. (London: Thorsons, 1996) pp. 3-15.

[20] Prudence Jones, "Pagan Theologies," in *Paganism Today: Wiccans, Druids, the Goddess and Ancient Earth Traditions for the Twenty-First Century*, Graham Harvey and Charlotte Hardman, eds. (London: Thorsons, 1996) pp. 32-34.

[21] I depend upon Oswalt for the term "continuity," who depends in turn on James Barr's identification of a "doctrine of correspondences" at work in paganism. Oswalt, *Bible among the Myths*, pp. 43-46; and James Barr, "The Meaning of 'mythology' in Relation to the Old Testament," *Vetus Testamentum* 9 (1959), pp. 5-6.

[22] As Susan Greenwood expresses it, "In short, divinity is immanent within anyone, the difference is that magicians are attuned to it." Greenwood, "The Magical Will, Gender, and Power in Magical Practices," *Paganism Today: Wiccans, Druids,*

the Goddess and Ancient Earth Traditions for the Twenty-First Century, Graham Harvey and Charlotte Hardman, eds. (London: Thorsons, 1996) p. 198.

[23] Gordon MacLellan, "Dancing on the Edge" *Paganism Today: Wiccans, Druids, the Goddess and Ancient Earth Traditions for the Twenty-First Century*, Graham Harvey and Charlotte Hardman, eds. (London: Thorsons, 1996) p. 147.

[24] Charlotte Hardman specifies love of nature and an embrace of the femininity of the divine as two of the three planks unifying most pagans. Hardman, "Introduction," in *Paganism Today: Wiccans, Druids, the Goddess and Ancient Earth Traditions for the Twenty-First Century*, Graham Harvey and Charlotte Hardman, eds. (London: Thorsons, 1996) p. xi.

[25] A definition and elaboration on the meta-divine can be found in Yehezkel Kaufmann, *The Religion of Israel: From its Beginnings to the Babylonian Exile*, translated and abridged by Moshe Greenberg (Chicago: University of Chicago Press, 1960), pp 22-24. I adopt the expression "the world-all" from Thomas Molnar, *The Pagan Temptation* (Grand Rapids: Eerdmans, 1987) p. 125.

[26] See Molnar's discussion on the loss of (divine) personhood in paganism; Ibid., pp. 61 and 124.

[27] Richard Sudcliffe, "Left-Hand Ritual Magick: An Historical and Philosophical Overview," in *Paganism Today: Wiccans, Druids, the Goddess and Ancient Earth Traditions for the Twenty-First Century*, Graham Harvey and Charlotte Hardman, eds. (London: Thorsons, 1996) p. 116.

[28] Antoine Faivre and Jacob Needleman, eds. *Modern Esoteric Spirituality* (London: SCM Press Ltd. 1993) p. xvi.

[29] Prudence Jones, "Pagan Theologies," pp. 39.

[30] The Pagan Federation. www.paganfederation.org.

[31] Prudence Jones, "Pagan Theologies," pp. 32.

[32] Shan Jayran, "Darklight Philosophy: A Ritual Practice," *Paganism Today: Wiccans, Druids, the Goddess and Ancient Earth Traditions for the Twenty-First Century*, Graham Harvey and Charlotte Hardman, eds. (London: Thorsons, 1996) p. 212.

[33] As an example (Egyptian) of how ancient Near Eastern understandings of creation envisioned this material continuity, see J. P. Allen, *Genesis in Egypt: The Philosophy of Ancient Egyptian Creation*, Yale Egyptological Studies 2 (New Haven: Yale University Press, 1988) pp. 13-14.

[34] At this point Mormonism sides with paganism. President Lorenzo Snow declared: "As man now is, God once was: as God is now, man may be." Similarly Joseph Smith, "God himself was once as we are now, and is an exalted man, and sits enthroned in yonder heavens! That is the great secret." See Stephen E. Robinson, "God the Father," in *Encyclopedia of Mormonism* (New York: MacMillan, 1992) p. 549.

[35] The congregational response "Thanks be to God" after the reading of scripture is a vivid acknowledgement of our fundamental need for God's self-revelation. Conversely, Charlotte Hardman characterizes paganism as "attacking Revelation," judging religions of (supernatural) revelation to be undermining "human autonomy and self-worth." Conversely, pagans are specially equipped to "challenge exclusivist claims," since pagans have access to "the Earth as a resource." Hardman, "Introduction," *Paganism Today: Wiccans, Druids, the Goddess and Ancient Earth Traditions for the Twenty-First Century*, Graham Harvey and Charlotte Hardman, eds. (London: Thorsons, 1996) p. xvii.

[36] The NT quotation in I Peter 1:16 depends on such passages as Leviticus 11:44-45, 19:2, and 20:7.

[37] Molnar laments the encroachment of imaginative new rites upon instituted rites, as if they bear equal weight with the latter. "Whatever has meaning in the eyes of this or that individual or group may be assimilated into the celebration since what counts is no longer the sacramental reality but the commemoration by whatever signs the group agrees upon." Molnar, *Pagan Temptation*, pp 192-93.

[38] Wesley's definition of the Means of Grace bears this out: "By "Means of Grace" I understand outward signs, words, or actions *ordained of God, and appointed for this end*, to be the ordinary channels whereby he might convey to men, preventing, justifying, or sanctifying grace." Wesley, "The Means of Grace" (Sermon XVI) V: 187. [Emphasis added]

[39] Wesley, "The Means of Grace" (sermon XVI) V: 200.

[40] Wesley, "The Means of Grace" (sermon XVI) V: 201.

[41] Wesley, "A Plain Account of Perfection" XI: 402-3.

[42] Wesley, "The Means of Grace" (sermon XVI) V: 201.

[43] Molnar argues eloquently: "[F]aith can arise only where there is a personal God.... [O]nly such [a personal, transcendent] God can call forth faith...". Molnar, *Pagan Temptation*, pp. 60-61.

Works Cited

Allen, J.P.
   1988   *Genesis in Egypt: The Philosophy of Ancient Egyptian Creation*, Yale Egyptological Studies 2. New Haven: Yale University Press.

Barr, James
   1959   "The Meaning of 'mythology' in Relation to the Old Testament," *Vetus Testamentum* 9, pp. 5-6.

Collins, Kenneth J. and Jason E. Vickers, eds.
   2013   The Sermons of John Wesley: A Collection for the Christian Journey. Nashville, TN: Abingdon.

Faivre, Antoine and Jacob Needleman, eds.
   1993   *Modern Esoteric Spirituality*. London: SCM Press Ltd.

Harvey, Graham and Charlotte Hardman, eds.
   1996   *Paganism Today: Wiccans, Druids, the Goddess and Ancient Earth Traditions for the Twenty-First Century*. London: Thorsons.

Kaufmann, Yehezkel
   1960   *The Religion of Israel: From its Beginnings to the Babylonian Exile*, translated and abridged by Moshe Greenberg. Chicago: University of Chicago Press.

Molnar, Thomas
   1987   *The Pagan Temptation*. Grand Rapids, MI: Eerdmans.

Oswalt, John N.
   2009   *The Bible among the Myths: Unique Revelation or Just Ancient Literature?* Grand Rapids, MI: Zondervan.

Pagan Federation
    Nd.   "What is Paganism" accessed on www.paganfederation.org.

Robinson, Stephen E.
    1992   "God the Father," in *Encyclopedia of Mormonism*. New York: MacMillan, p. 549.

Wesley, John
    1872   "The Character of a Methodist," in *The Works of John Wesley*, Thomas Jackson ed., 3rd Edition. London: Wesleyan Conference Office.

Isaiah's Model House

NANCY ERICKSON

KEYWORDS:

Isaiah, model house/shrine, idol fashioning, archaeology, shared cognitive environment

Nancy Erickson (PhD, Hebrew Union College-Jewish Institute of Religion) is Senior Editor of Biblical Languages, Textbooks, and Reference Tools at Zondervan Academic. She is coeditor and contributor of *Windows to the Ancient World of the Hebrew Bible: Essays in Honor of Samuel Greengus* (Eisenbrauns, 2014).

ABSTRACT

Isaiah's scrutiny of idol fashioning in 44:6–20 provides a window into his understanding of image making in the ancient Near East. The prophet's descriptions are a symptom of his shared perception, or the common cognitive environment, of the ancient world in which he lived; this includes information gathered from the discipline of biblical archaeology. Based on the cultic literary context of Isaiah 44, a nuance of the usual meaning of the Hebrew term בית, and the prophet's larger shared environment attested by the material culture of the ancient Near East, I suggest Isaiah's use of בית in 44:13b assumes a "model house."

INTRODUCTION

At the core of archaeological work is the hope of uncovering the past. Unearthed material provides a window to worlds gone by, a glimpse into ancient civilizations and millennia of evolution, and the possibility of examining history through its own lens. For Biblicists, archaeology may illumine the biblical texts and provide material comment to an ancient worldview.

In the nineteenth century a surplus of archaeological data, both textual and material, from Egypt, Mesopotamia, and Syria-Palestine created enormous enthusiasm among biblical scholars. Such was the excitement that copious analogues between biblical Israel and the ancient Near East led to an abuse of comparative studies between ancient cultures. The exaggeration of parallels was something S. Sandmel aptly labeled "parallelomania."[1] Since then biblical scholars have developed a more nuanced framework with which to interpret material culture of the ancient Near East and the biblical testament.[2] Notably, in a series of essays Hallo has proposed a "contextual method," which seeks to observe the convergences as well as the divergences in ancient Near Eastern literature and culture with the Hebrew Bible.[3] Other scholars have further nuanced Hallo's contextual approach.[4]

For the purposes of this essay I would like to highlight Walton's nuance of the contextual approach in what he labels a "common cognitive environment," that is, the thought world that ancient Israel shared with surrounding cultures.[5] The theory assumes that neighboring peoples in the ancient Near East were in contact with one another and simply shared a cultural milieu. This is not to say that distinctiveness was lost (although determining ethnicity and/or people groups such as ancient Israel is a particularly daunting task when recovering the past) but rather that the unique identity of peoples allowed for comment, both textual and material, of the same shared environment. Walton's approach is not particularly different from Hallo's contextual approach but it does highlight a certain fluidity when discussing known or accepted practices in the ancient world without necessarily indicating such beliefs or practices were adopted. Just as I can speak freely and with a fair amount of knowledge about football even though I have never played the sport, so too our biblical writers wrote freely about the world in which they lived. It is with this theoretical framework in mind that I would like to address Isaiah's understanding of בית in 44:13b.[6]

Below I will first address the larger biblical text of Isaiah 44:6–20, noting its salient literary features and some intricacies in translation, and then I will move into a discussion of verse 13b and the Hebrew term בית. I will then summarize pertinent archaeological finds to provide a background for Isaiah's shared cognitive environment that will help inform the prophet's understanding of בית.

ISAIAH 44:6–20

Isaiah's oracle of YHWH (כה־אמר יהוה) in 44:6–20 is a scrutiny of idol fashioning. The message moves from self-declaration (מבלעדי אין אלהים, "There is no god beside me," v. 6) and rhetorical questioning (מי־כמוני, "Who is like me?" v. 7) in verses 6–8 to harsh critique and mockery of image-makers in verses 9–20. The message has clear linguistic and thematic echoes across the biblical canon. Consider YHWH's rhetorical questioning of Job in chapters 38–40, perhaps most poignantly, "Who has put wisdom in the innermost being? Who has given understanding to the mind?" (38:7), and similar phrasing throughout the book of Isaiah (see 40:18, 25; 41:26). Descriptions of a critique of idol worship and fashioning may be noted in Deuteronomy 4. On the plains of Moab, Moses reminds his audience to watch themselves (שמר) lest they be inclined to fashion images in direct prohibition of the covenant YHWH made on Mt. Horeb (4:15, 23). Image fashioning is prohibited in YHWH's cult, yet it is a constant struggle for our ancient heroes and a source of regular discussion among our biblical writers (i.e., Lev 18:30; Deut 7:26; 12:31; Ezek 7:20; Isa 1:13; 40:18–20; 41:24). Surely the content of Isaiah 44:6–20 is at home for our prophet and perhaps nowhere else in the biblical corpus is the issue so extensively and systematically critiqued.

Before taking up the details of verses 6–20, consider the larger context of 44:21–28. Lexical repetition ties these later verses with the earlier section in 6–20 and hammers home the prophet's theological message: YHWH alone creates (v. 21, 24–28) and he redeems (vv. 22, 23, 24; גאל). With the foolishness of idol fashioning in mind (vv. 6–20), YHWH calls his audience to "remember … return to me, for I have redeemed you" (vv. 21 and 22; זכר … שובה אלי כי גאלתיך). The prophet's message is all the more poignant following the mockery of images and their makers in verses 6–20.

The literary styling of verses 6–20 may be considered quasi poetic. Some Hebrew parallelism is apparent in the section: 6–8, 9–11 and 18–20. But verses 12–17 appear to be lacking poetic construction in the same sense. Watts nonetheless presents his entire translation in poetry, identifying individual stichs.[7] *BHS* also displays the text as poetry. Berlin identifies a unique sound pair (of consonance) in verse 8 (בלעדי and בל ידעתי) that she sees elsewhere in the biblical canon only twice (2 Sam 22:32; Ps 18:32).[8] Oswalt labels the entire section of 9–20 as "somewhat prosaic."[9] Differing opinions on the literary style of 6–20 are a testament to the difficulty of translation and interpretation of the passage.[10]

The specific descriptions of idol fashioning fall in verses 12–17 and seem to appear in unusual order causing some to suggest the prophet has reversed the steps of image making.[11] The process is described as follows: the ironsmith shapes and forges his work with tools and strength (v. 12) yet he grows hungry and weak; the carpenter measures, designs, and fashions the image in the form of a man for residing in a house (v. 13); the wood materials are acquired (in 14a the cutting of wood seems to precede the growing in 14b); some of the wood is used for fuel while the other is made into an image that is worshiped (v. 15); half of the wood is used for meal preparation and warmth (v. 16); the other half of the wood is used for fashioning a god to whom the craftsman worships and prays (v. 17). Certainly the sequencing of the steps is obscured for the reader but perhaps a logical order was not Isaiah's aim. Regardless it is clear that the prophet is well-versed in how image makers operate, their tools that they use, and their general method for creation. Childs notes that the prophet's details reveal careful firsthand observations "rather than being simply a catena of stereotyped caricatures of idolatry that had long since floated loose from any concrete historical experience."[12]

Verses 6–20 are littered with difficult vocabulary and syntax (in addition to the uneasy chronological order and question of literary style noted above). I will highlight here just a few elements of interest and then move to a discussion of the Hebrew term בית in verse 13b. The *hapax legomenon* in verse 8, תִּרְהוּ, is difficult. Its meaning is based primarily on the parallel with פחד, "trembling, dread, fear" and Arabic *wariha*.[13] Presumably relying on this parallel, 1QIsᵃ reads תיראו, "fear." The dots over המה in verse 9 are of particular interest. They are called *puncta extraordinaria*, "extraordinary/special points," and seem to indicate uncertainty or reservation from the scribes.[14] The rare term in verse 12, מעצד, also occurs in Jeremiah 10:3 as a tool for woodwork. A fine translation seems to be "small axe."[15]

Others have favored haplography here, where גל has fallen out, there rendering עצד גלם, "he cuts out a mould," but this seems unnecessary.[16] The *qere* יְסָגוֹד in verse 17 is suggested by the Mp for *ketiv* יְסְגָּד.

Verse 13 presents its own challenges for translation. Six verbal forms seem to pile up: נָטָה, יְתָאֲרֵהוּ, יַעֲשֵׂהוּ, יְתָאֲרֵהוּ, יַעֲשֵׂהוּ, and לְשֶׁבֶת. Note the repetition of roots and forms. The LXX renders the verse shorter, leaving out the repetition. The movement of verbal aspect is noted by Oswalt, suggesting it lends to the difficulty of translation for the verse.[17] Most English translations render verse 13 as a gnomic present (NASB, NIV, CEB, et al.). Oswalt comments the variation is a way for the prophet to "convey immediacy," where some of the project is complete while some of the project is still on going.[18] The word שֶׂרֶד in the second stich of verse 13 (following יְתָאֲרֵהוּ) is a *hapax legomenon* with a fascinating history.[19] Evidently a misunderstanding by later (Middle Ages) Hebrew philologists of the medieval Arabic translation of the Bible by Saadya Gaon prompted meanings related to a red-dyed cord though Saadya had translated the noun as a carpenter's plane.[20] The mistake influenced Jewish interpretation, which in turn influenced Christian biblical exegetes and modern scholarship. NASB translates the noun "red chalk." Probably a better rendering of the *hapax* is related to the carpenter's plane, as Saadya suggests, or perhaps a similar sharp stylus.[21] The form מקצעות is also a *hapax*. Its meaning is assumed from the root קצע and is best understood as a utensil for cutting or scraping, perhaps "carving tool" as the CEB translates.[22]

The ל + infinitive construction in 13b, לְשֶׁבֶת, may express the result of the many actions of the entire verse (see above, though this is difficult) and this is how some translations render the infinitive, "*so that* it may dwell" in a house (i.e., NASB, NIV). Other translations render the infinitive more loosely, "*to* dwell" in a house (NRSV, CEB, Watts). The full expression with the infinitive is לְשֶׁבֶת בָּיִת, something like "for dwelling/to dwell a house." The clumsy English rendering follows the Hebrew. The LXX adds the dative preposition ἐν to ease the translation, "to dwell/set up *in* a house." English translations follow (i.e., NASB, NRSV, NIV, Watts, Childs, Oswalt, etc.) and this seems to be the best meaning. The assumed object of the expression is labeled with two descriptions in verse 10: פֶּסֶל, אֵל, "god," "idol/image." Subsequently, it is a deity or idol that is envisioned as residing *in* the house of 13b.

The noun בית in 13b is ubiquitous in the Hebrew Bible. Its semantic range includes "dwelling," in its various facets, and "family," as in a family line/house. The noun is also used in numerous compound place names, such as בֵּית־אֵל, "Bethel."[23] The semantic range in the Hebrew Bible for the definition related to "dwelling" is not particularly broad; it means "house" with its many nuances just like the English term (i.e., mansion, cabin, tent, container, mouse-hole, etc.). Sometimes the term is specified: the abode, or "house," of a spider i.e., "spider's web" (Job 8:14), a "bird nest" (Ps 84:4[3]; 104:17), or a habitat for moths (Job 27:18). In cultic contexts בית may refer specifically to a "house" of a god, or by extension "temple."[24] Exodus 23:19 denotes בית אלהים, "*house* of God"; 1 Samuel 5:2 describes a בית דגון, "*house* of Dagon"; 2 Samuel 12:20 reads בית יהוה, "*house* of YHWH"; and there are many other examples (i.e., Gen 28:22; Judg 17:4–5 and 18:31; 1 Sam 1:7; 1 Kgs 8:10; 2 Kgs 10:25; 2 Chron 34:9). The meaning of בית in Isaiah 44:13 falls within this range of interpretation: a house/abode of a deity/idol for dwelling. Below I suggest that the particular nuance of the noun (missing from the standard lexicons) that Isaiah imagines in 44:13b indicates a "*model* house/abode" for a deity, such as those attested in the archaeological record of the ancient Near East.

Model Houses/Shrines in the Ancient Near East

Model houses/shrines from the ancient Near East are a well-known phenomenon. Such model houses are known from the third millennium onward and attested from a wide geographical area. There is little question that the model shrines were used for cultic purposes. Their contexts, in or near temples or rooms with clear cultic activity, and decorations (more on this below) support the assumption. The general shape of the models is either rectangular, with a small floor area and larger wall, or rounded, appearing like a jar thrown on a potter's wheel with an incised door. Interestingly, some extant shrines have yielded evidence of a closing device near the opening, indicating that a door did not survive. The model house from Tel Rekhesh (ninth century) attests indications of such a door (two holes on the right side of the opening of the receptacle) and was likely used as a box to hold a divine figure.[25] This assumption may be supported by other models such as the older, well-known Ashkelon shrine (ca. seventeenth century) with accompanying calf. As with the model at Tel Rekhesh, the Ashkelon model attests evidence of a clay closure and in this instance, the resident figure (calf) was found *in situ* with the model.[26] Extant examples such as these confirm one possible function of model houses, that is to "house" a deity or image/idol.

16th century BCE model shrine and accompanying calf from Ashkelon

(Credit: Kim Walton from the Israel Museum, Used with Permission)

Other extant shrines attest a simple opening on one end with no assumed door or closing feature. Many of these shrines, however, demonstrate decorative elements on the façade such as pillars, trees, lions, doves, or deities/figurines; iconography that is familiar to ancient Near Eastern cultic contexts.[27] Such stylized façades may have functioned to identify the deity/deities with the shrine and so are considered iconic, lacking a portable figurine but detailing identification through affixed stylized art. Some model shrines demonstrate a more simplistic styling and may be considered aniconic, lacking a likeness of a deity but by representation through something associated with a deity considered a sign of the deity's presence. The terracotta model shrine from Akhziv (seventh century; Phoenician mainland) is one such example. Quoting Culican, Doak states that the piece was a "'deliberate attempt' to create an 'aniconic cult object.'"[28]

9th-8th century BCE model shrine from Jordan

(Credit: Kim Walton from the Israel Museum, Used with Permission)

Many scholars classify the model house/shrines as miniaturizations of larger scale edifices such as temples.[29] For Ziony Zevit, this connection between a model and its larger, cultic version is crucial for understanding the shrine's functions.[30] However, identifying the larger representation of so many varying, smaller models is a difficult if not impossible task. Nonetheless, we can be quite certain that these small, house-shaped shrines are related to the cult and many, if not all, were considered a type of dwelling or "house" for a deity/deities.[31] The larger repertoire of these model houses, just a few of which are noted here, were certainly a part of the shared cognitive environment of the writer of Isaiah 44:13b (cf. the model houses from Ugarit, Dan, Tirzah, Hazor, Gezer, Transjordan, and elsewhere).[32] Which type of model house the prophet had in mind is unknown but perhaps one similar to those attesting a door, intended to house an image or idol like one whose manufacturing is described in verses 12–14.

In an attempt to find such model houses/shrines in the biblical texts Zevit proposes that the rare biblical word חמן, found in Ezekiel 6:6 and 2 Chronicles 34:4, in fact refers to the miniaturized construction. The term is usually translated "incense altar" (i.e., CEB, NASB, NIV, NRSV). Zevit's conclusion is cautious but he may be correct.[33] The term is not well understood.[34] Even if Zevit's suggestion for understanding חמן is correct I propose that the writer of Isaiah utilized the term בית in 44:13b to mean a model house/shrine; the prophet would not have been bound to a single expression. Indeed, Isaiah is littered with varied and colorful vocabulary. The rendering of בית as a "model house" of a deity/idol is supported by the cultic literary context, the semantic range of the term בית, and the larger shared environment attested by the material culture of the ancient Near East.[35]

CONCLUDING REMARKS

Isaiah's use of בית in 44:13b is included among one of the most thorough treatments scrutinizing images and their fashioners in the Hebrew Bible. The term is easily translated "house" and includes a range of related nuancing. I suggest that the particular type of house that the prophet has in mind is not unlike one of the many model houses/shrines extant in the ancient Near East. Such models were certainly a part of Isaiah's common cognitive environment and the prophet freely drew upon this assumed knowledge when describing the residence of the idols he so skillfully mocks.

POSTSCRIPT

My hope when I began this essay was seeded in reaction to current scholarship, at least as I perceive it. There is a tendency in any field for the proverbial pendulum to swing far in one direction just to swing back in the other and I have sensed recently in the field of biblical studies a certain fear among scholars to once again delve into the cultural milieu of the ancient Near East. As academics we become so focused in our study that we easily become a student of the text or rather, a student of the material culture.[36] While it used to be that Biblicists over-emphasized similarities between ancient Israel and surrounding cultures it seems now that the shared worldview has been missing in many a discussion. I hope here to offer a small contribution to further understand the multi-faceted worldview of our biblical prophet.

END NOTES

¹ S. Sandmel, "Parallelomania," *JBL* 81 (1962):1–13.

² Nuances have developed over time, from such interpretations as those supported by Friedrich Delitzsch, whose famous lectures, "Babel und Bibel," (delivered January 13, 1902, January 12, 1903, and October 18 and 27, 1904) suggested that ancient Israel was essentially derivative of Babylon without uniqueness, to Benno Landsberger's response, proposing that Babylon should be investigated on her own terms (Benno Landsberger, "Die Eigenbegrifflichkeit der babylonischen Welt," *Islamica* 2 [1926]: 355–72). For a review see Peter Machinist, "Assyriology and the Bible: Benno Landsberger's *Eigenbegrifflichkeit* Revisited," SBL annual meeting paper (Atlanta, GA, November 23, 2003); see also Bill T. Arnold and David B. Weisberg, "A Centennial Review of Friedrich Delitzsch's 'Babel und Bibel' Lectures," *JBL* 121/3 (2002): 441–57, for a review of Delitzsch's work.

³ Hallo first introduced the comparative methodology in his article "New Viewpoints on Cuneiform Literature," *IEJ* 12 (1962): 13–26. He has since written numerous articles on the subject, as have many others. Here I highlight just a few: Hallo, "Biblical History in its Near Eastern Setting: The Contextual Approach," in *Essays on the Comparative Method*, eds. W. Hallo, Carl D. Evans, John Bradley White, SIC I (Pittsburg: Pickwick Press, 1980), 1–26; "Compare and Contrast: The Contextual Approach to Biblical Literature," in *The Bible in the Light of Cuneiform Literature*, eds. W. Hallo, Bruce W. Jones, Gerald L. Mattingly, SIC III (New York: E. Mellen Press, 1990), 1–30; K. Lawson Younger, Jr., "The 'Contextual Method': Some West Semitic Reflections," in *The Context of Scripture: Archival Documents from the Biblical World*, vol. 3 (Leiden: Brill, 2002), xxxv–xlii; S. Parker, Stories in *Scripture and Inscriptions: Comparative Studies on Narratives in Northwest Semitic Inscriptions and the Hebrew Bible* (New York: Oxford University Press, 1997).

⁴ Many a method are espoused in numerous works that deal with comparative studies but see especially, M. Malul, *Comparative Method in Ancient Near Eastern and Biblical Legal Texts*, AOAT 227 (Kevelaer: Butzon and Bercker, 1990) and Jack M. Sasson, "About 'Mari and the Bible'," *RA* 92 (1998): 97–123, esp. 98–99.

[5] John Walton, *Ancient Near Eastern Thought and the Old Testament: Introducing the Conceptual World of the Hebrew Bible* (Grand Rapids: Baker, 2006).

[6] My interest in Isaiah is in hope of honoring John Oswalt and his many published works that address the prophet.

[7] John D. W. Watts, *Isaiah 34–66*, WBC 25, rev. ed. (Nashville: Thomas Nelson, 2000), 680–82.

[8] Adele Berlin, *The Dynamics of Biblical Parallelism* (Bloomington: Indiana University Press, 1985), 105–06. Berlin also identifies a phonological repetition in verses 6 and 9 that she ties to verse 8.

[9] John N. Oswalt, *The Book of Isaiah: Chapter 40–66*, NICOT (Grand Rapids: Eerdmans, 1998), 170.

[10] The question of the literary style of verses 9–20 and the seemingly otherwise connectedness between verses 6–8 and 21–23 have prompted some scholars to assume the section is a late addition. Oswalt confirms its unity. See his discussion, 170-88.

[11] Oswalt, 180.

[12] Brevard S. Childs, *Isaiah*, OTL (Louisville: Westminster John Knox Press, 2001), 343.

[13] *HALOT* 1:436.

[14] Gary V. Smith, *Isaiah 40–66*, NAC 15b (Nashville: Broadman & Holman, 2009), 230. 1QIs[a] places the term above the line, apparently a later addition. Some fifteen examples of *puncta extraordinaria* occur in the Hebrew Bible.

[15] *HALOT* 1:615.

[16] Watts, 684–85. Following the tradition of WBC Watts has a full technical discussion on the many unique forms and variants of our passage. See 683–685.

[17] Oswalt, 178.

[18] Ibid.

[19] Note that the same root vocalized differently appears elsewhere in the Hebrew Bible to refer to woven or embroidered clothing (Exod 31:10; 35:19). The meaning hardly makes sense here. *HALOT* 2:1354.

[20] Joshua Blau, "A Misunderstood Medieval Translation of *śered* (Isaiah 44:13) and its Impact on Modern Scholarship," in *Pomegranates and Golden Bells: Studies in Biblical, Jewish, and Near Eastern ritual, Law, and Literature in Honor of Jacob Milgraom*, ed. D. P. Wright et al. (Winona Lake, IN: Eisenbrauns, 1995), 689–95.

[21] *HALOT* 2:1354

[22] *HALOT* 1:628, 2:1123–24.

[23] See *HALOT* 1:124–29 for the full entry. Cf. *TDOT* 2:107–13; *NIDOTTE* 1:655–57.

[24] *HALOT* 1:124.

[25] Yosef Garfinkel and Madeleine Mumcuoglu, "A Shrine Model from Tel Rekhesh," *Bulletin of the Anglo-Israel Archaeological Society* 33 (2015): 77–87. The dating of the Tel Rekhesh model is based on part by comparison with a similar shrine discovered at Tel Rehov, also dated to the Iron Age IIA.

[26] Lawrence Stager, "When Canaanites and Philistines Ruled Ashkelon," *BAR* 17.2 (1991): 24–43.

[27] One of the more recently discussed model shrines appears to come from the north-central Cisjordan or northern Transjordan region from the Iron Age II period (so Aren Maeir and Michal Dayagi-Mendels, "An Elaborately Decorated Clay Model Shrine from the Moussaeiff Collection," *Images as Sources: Studies on ancient Near Eastern artefacts and the Bible inspired by the work of Othmar Keel, Orbis Biblicus et Orientalis*, special vol., [2007]: 111–124). The shrine's complex decorations are reason for the discussion and include a recumbent lion, applied female figurines, and stylized columns.

[28] Brian R. Doak, *Phoenician Aniconism in Its Mediterranean and Ancient Near Eastern Contexts* (Atlanta: SBL Press, 2015), 105. For William Culican's article see, "A Terracotta Shrine from Achzib," *ZDPV* 92 (1976): 47–53.

29 The term "miniaturization" seems to have been first used by Claude Lévi-Strauss (*The Savage Mind* [Chicago: University of Chicago Press, 1966], 23–25) followed by Jonathan Z. Smith ("Trading Places," in *Relating Religion: Essays in the Study of Religion* [Chicago: University of Chicago Press, 2004], 215–29) but see Doak, 102.

30 Ziony Zevit, *The Religions of Ancient Israel: A Synthesis of Parallactic Approaches* (New York: Continuum, 2001), 328–43. Doak describes Zevit's endeavor as guesswork, 103.

31 Maier and Dayagi-Mendels, 117–18.

32 Zevit, 328-338.

33 Zevit, 340.

34 *HALOT* 1:329.

35 I acknowledge that the prophet may have intended for 13b to be understood differently, that the image was made for dwelling in *someone's* house, perhaps in the *idol-fashioner's* house. Goldingay and Payne follow this interpretation. They are bound to their rendering of בית as an adverb, "at home," and subsequently take the entire clause to indicate that the idol was "domesticated" (John Goldingay and David Payne, *Isaiah* 40–55, 2 vols., ICC [New York: T&T Clark, 2006, 353–54]).

36 One readily available symptom of this split in academic fields can be seen in the absence of biblical scholars present at meetings devoted to material culture. While ETS, SBL, and AAR members happily engage and attend meetings related to theology and literature, ASOR members happily dialogue with one another in a different part of town. (This was quite literally the case at the most recent annual meetings in San Antonio, 2016.) The disciplines reap maximal benefit when in discussion with one another but sadly this is often not the case. The advantage is not limited to just literature and material culture, consider philosophy, the sciences, anthropology, sociology, etc.

Works Cited

Berlin, Adele
1985   *The Dynamics of Biblical Parallelism.* Bloomington, IN: Indiana University Press.

Blau, Joshua
1995   "A Misunderstood Medieval Translation of *śered* (Isaiah 44:13) and its Impact on Modern Scholarship." Pages 689–95 in *Pomegranates and Golden Bells: Studies in Biblical, Jewish, and Near Eastern ritual, Law, and Literature in Honor of Jacob Milgraom.* Edited by D. P. Wright et al. Winona Lake, IN: Eisenbrauns.

Childs, Brevard S.
2001   *Isaiah.* OTL. Louisville: Westminster John Knox Press.

Doak, Brian R.
2015   *Pheonician Aniconism in Its Mediterranean and Ancient Near Eastern Contexts.* Atlanta: SBL Press.

Garfinkel, Yosef and Madeleine Mumcuoglu
2015   "A Shrine Model from Tel Rekhesh," *Bulletin of the Anglo-Israel Archaeological Society* 33: 77–87.

Goldingay, John and David Payne
2006   *Isaiah 40–55,* 2 vols., ICC. New York: T&T Clark.

Maeir, Aren and Michal Dayagi-Mendels
2007   "An Elaborately Decorated Clay Model Shrine from the Moussaeiff Collection," *Images as Sources: Studies on ancient Near Eastern artefacts and the Bible inspired by the work of Othmar Keel, Orbis Biblicus et Orientalis,* special vol.: 111–24.

Oswalt, John N.
    1998   *The Book of Isaiah: Chapter 40–66.* NICOT. Grand Rapids: Eerdmans.

Sandmel, S.
    1962   "Parallelomania," *JBL* 81:1–13.

Smith, Gary V.
    2009   *Isaiah 40–66.* NAC 15b. Nashville: Broadman & Holman.

Stager, Lawrence
    1991   "When Canaanites and Philistines Ruled Ashkelon," *BAR* 17.2: 24–43.

Walton, John
    2006   *Ancient Near Eastern Thought and the Old Testament: Introducing the Conceptual World of the Hebrew Bible.* Grand Rapids: Baker.

Watts, John D. W.
    2000   *Isaiah 34–66.* WBC 25. Rev. ed. Nashville: Thomas Nelson.

Zevit, Ziony
    2001   *The Religions of Ancient Israel: A Synthesis of Parallactic Approaches.* New York: Continuum.

A Prophet Unlike Moses: Balaam as Prophetic Intercessor

L. Daniel Hawk

KEYWORDS:

Balaam, Moses, prophecy, intercession, Book of Numbers

L. Daniel Hawk (PhD, Emory University) is Professor of Old Testament and Hebrew at Ashland Theological Seminary, in Ashland, Ohio

Abstract

The Balaam narrative (Numbers 22:1-24:25) is fraught with textual and theological incongruity. A narrative analysis of the corpus, however, reveals the incongruities as literary devices that render Balaam as a prophetic anti-type in contrast to Moses. While both Balaam and Moses are obedient messengers who speak the words of YHWH, their ministry as intercessors manifests vastly different understandings of YHWH. Both figures try to change YHWH's mind. Balaam does so through ritual manipulation and with the idea that YHWH can be induced to curse what YHWH has blessed. Moses, however, directly appeals to YHWH for mercy in response to a divine decree of destruction. The prominence and ambiguous rendering of the Balaam narrative therefore reflects its importance in assisting Israel to discern trustworthy versus untrustworthy prophets.

Introduction

The Balaam narrative (Numbers 22:2-24:25) is a jumble of anomalies. It begins by presenting Balaam as an exemplary servant of YHWH. Balaam consults YHWH for direction when emissaries from the Moabite king Balak seek his aid to curse Israel (22:8). He does not go with them when YHWH forbids him to go (22:10). When emissaries with more prestige arrive and tell him to name his own price, he emphatically declares that he cannot go beyond what God has commanded him (22:16-18). Then he departs, in obedience to YHWH's command that he accompany them (22:20-21). Immediately following, however, we read that God is enraged that Balaam goes with the men and that the angel of YHWH blocks his way (22:22-24). The story takes a farcical turn, as a donkey sees what the prophet cannot and questions him (22:25-30), only to have the angel rebuke Balaam for his crooked way and inform the prophet that the donkey has saved his life (22:31-33). After the angel admonishes him to say only what YHWH tells him to say, the narrative again depicts him as an exemplary servant; Balaam declares that he cannot be bought and will only say what YHWH tells him (23:12-13, 26; 24:12-13).

There are also inconsistencies of broader import. What is a non-Israelite diviner doing delivering prophecies in the name of YHWH? How is Balaam on speaking terms with YHWH? How does Balaam even know the divine name, disclosed to Moses only a generation earlier (Exod 6:2-3)? And why does Numbers devote so much attention to a pagan prophet?

Subsequent biblical references to Balaam take a neutral or negative slant. In most cases Balaam appears in connection with Balak's attempt to curse Israel (Deut 23:4-5; Josh 24:9-10; Mic 6:4). Two reports that the Israelites killed Balaam along with the kings of Midian cast him as an enemy (Num 31:8; Josh 13:22). Two additional references in the New Testament paint an even darker picture. Second Peter presents Balaam as an example of avarice (2:15). Revelation 2:14, on the other hand, depicts Balaam as a sinister seducer who taught Balak to draw the Israelites into idolatry and fornication.

Early Christian and Jewish interpretation echoes the ambiguous character of the biblical narrative. Ambrose viewed Balaam as proud man who was motivated by the love of money. Jerome, on the other hand, wondered why Balaam was able to see the coming of Christ more clearly than many prophets, and an array of interpreters associated his prophecy of a star coming from Jacob (24:17) with the star that guided the Magi – other outsiders to whom God spoke (Lienhard 2001:243-49).

Early rabbinic interpretation generally casts Balaam in a negative light, with a prominent thread corresponding to the Christian depiction of Balaam as proud, greedy, seductive, and mendacious (b. Sanh. 105a-b; b. Sanh. 106a.); one tradition casts him as a figure of archetypal wickedness characterized by an evil eye, an arrogant spirit and a proud soul, and leading a host of followers to Gehenna (m. 'Abot 5:19). Another thread contrasts Moses with Balaam as an exercise of differentiating Israel's prophets from those of the rest of the world. One positive perspective renders Balaam as a prophet to the nations, in contrast to Moses as a prophet to Israel, and identifies the qualities that distinguished them (Num. Rab. 14:20). A negative comparison, on the other hand, contrasts the compassion and message of Israel's prophets with the cruelty of pagan Balaam, who wanted to destroy an entire nation without cause (Num. Rab. 20:1).

Extending this last thread of rabbinic midrash, in its opposing strands, into narrative analysis, reveals that the Balaam narrative renders its protagonist as a sort of prophetic anti-type in contrast to Moses. Both Moses and Balaam are depicted as obedient servants of YHWH who speak YHWH's words. Yet Moses is an exemplary figure, while Balaam is ultimately false and dangerous. On what basis is this distinction made? The answer, the story suggests, is to be discerned in the way that Balaam undertakes the task of prophetic intercession. The story of Balaam, in brief, presents an opposing depiction of prophetic ministry, rendered to assist Israel in the task of distinguishing between true messengers and the false ones. Balaam manifests many of the attributes of a true prophet of YHWH. Yet Balaam undertakes intercession, a primary prophetic task, in a radically different way than Moses, and in so doing reveals what characterizes untrustworthy prophets.

PRIESTHOOD AND PROPHECY IN NUMBERS

Israel in Numbers is an ordered and ordering community wandering within a boundless wasteland. Ordering the life of Israel, particularly in terms of its social manifestations, constitutes a prominent motif in the book. Numbers begins with an ordering event, a census and registration of the people according to tribe, clan, and patriarchal household (1:1-47). Another ordering event follows: a schematic configuration of the Israelite camp, in which the tribes are assigned places facing the tent of meeting on every side, under tribal ensigns and according to tribes, clans, and patriarchal households (2:1-34). There follows in turn a delineation of Levitical duties (3:5-13), a corresponding census and placement of Levites within the Israelite camps according to clans, and an assignment of responsibilities relative to the tabernacle and altar, all according to clans (3:14-39; 4:1-49). After a brief section of legislation (5:1-6:21), the ordering impulse resumes with a detailed account of the presentation of offerings by the leaders of the twelve tribes (7:1-88) and the separation and consecration of the Levites (8:5-26).

With Israel's departure from Sinai (9:1-10:36), the book turns toward to a straightforward narrative mode and to the introduction of the prophetic office, the other institution of divine mediation in Israel (11:1-17). An instance of complaining, first from the people and then from Moses, provides the context for an outbreak of prophecy. In response to Moses's exasperated protest that he cannot shoulder the weight of leadership alone, YHWH declares that he will take some of the spirit in Moses and disperse it to seventy elders. Ensuing events depict various aspects of prophetic ministry, beginning with a dialogue between YHWH and Moses that ends with YHWH declaring, "Now you will see whether or not my word will take place" (v. 23). When YHWH puts some of Moses' spirit on the elders, they prophesy (v. 25). The prophesying spills over established protocol; the spirit rests on two men designated to receive it but who are not present with the others (v. 26). In response to Joshua's plea that Moses stop the disorderly situation, Moses declares that he wishes all the people were prophets (vv. 28-29). YHWH then fulfills his word with a miraculous provision of quails but follows this up with a plague (vv. 31-34).

The topic of YHWH's revelation to the prophet is then taken up in the next episode, which is precipitated by Miriam's opposition to Moses' marriage to a Cushite (12:1-10). The challenge provokes YHWH to summon Miriam the prophet, Aaron the priest, and Moses to the tent of meeting. Here YHWH speaks about prophets, elevates the singular status of Moses above all religious offices, and rebukes Miriam and Aaron. The encounter concludes with Moses interceding on behalf of a leprous Miriam and YHWH's mitigation of her status to a seven-day exclusion from the camp. The themes of opposition to Moses, Mosaic mediation, and divine judgment then extend into the next two events. First, when the people refuse to enter Canaan, Moses intercedes to turn away divine anger, and YHWH lessens the judgment he declared (13:1-14:45). Second, when Korah leads a rebellion against Moses, Moses appeals to God for vindication, and YHWH renders judgment upon the rebels (16:1-50).

A third iteration of the themes occurs during an episode at Meribah, shortly before the Balaam narrative (20:1-13). The account anticipates the story of Balaam in its allusion to magic. At Meribah, the people's complaining so vexes Moses that he strikes the rock in a manner that suggests a magical performance. By announcing that he and Aaron will bring water from the rock and then striking it twice, Moses signals that the miraculous power to do so issues from himself, rather than YHWH. For this, YHWH disqualifies Moses from leading the people into the land, "because he did not remain faithful to YHWH, to treat YHWH as holy in the sight of the people."[1] The performance undercuts YHWH's holiness by suggesting that YHWH is not truly transcendent and, like all the other deities of the ancient world, may be manipulated by someone with access to the superior power of magic.

BALAAM AS INTERCESSOR

Although Balaam is nowhere identified as a prophet, the narrative associates him with prophetic attributes and practices. He relays messages that YHWH gives him or puts in his mouth (22:8, 38; 23:5, 12, 16; 24:4; cf. 24:15), and two of his prophecies are specifically called oracles (24:4,15). He prophesies under the impulse of the divine spirit (24:2). Balaam evokes the visionary aspect of Israelite prophecy by referring to himself as one who sees with open and uncovered eyes, possesses the knowledge of the Most High, and he receives visions from the Almighty (24:4, 15, 16). He thereby casts himself as a seer, an alternative and perhaps archaic designation for a prophet (1 Sam 9:9, 19; 2 Sam 24:11; 2 Sam 17:13; Amos 7:12). The association is accentuated through irony in the satirical account of his donkey's stubbornness, during which the donkey sees what Balaam cannot and warns Balaam accordingly (22:21-35).

Balaam, however, is also associated with divination and sorcery. The Moabite and Midianite elders who approach Balaam on Balak's behalf believe him to be a diviner (22:7); that is, someone skilled in predicting the future and determining the divine will by reading omens or performing rituals. Balak, however, is not interested in knowing the future but in changing it. He enlists Balaam as a sorcerer, that is, someone who is able to wield transcendent power for good or ill. The Moabite king expects Balaam to curse Israel and becomes increasingly frustrated when Balaam repeatedly blesses the nation instead. The interplay between the roles of diviner and sorcerer has elicited significant discussion. The majority of interpreters regard sorcery as within the diviner's purview. Balaam's failure is therefore viewed in terms of YHWH's refusal to authorize the execration, and Balak's frustration emanates from his anger that he is not getting the diviner he paid for.[2] Jacob Milgrom, however, has argued that diviners and sorcerers were distinct and separate functionaries in northern Mesopotamia, the place of Balaam's residence. On this basis, Milgrom argues that Balak's frustration emanates from the fact that he wanted a sorcerer but hired a diviner.[3]

It is important to note at this point, however, that Balaam does little by way of action to confirm either of these roles. His divining consists only of looking for a favorable omen during the first two sacrifices (24:1). Likewise, he possesses the power to bless and curse only by reputation (22:6); Balaam himself repeatedly declares that he has no power to override YHWH's pronouncement of blessing over Israel (22:18, 38; 23:8, 12, 20; 24:12-13). In short, Balaam acts like a diviner, just as he acts as a prophet, but the office is never ascribed to him directly.

The first section of the narrative portrays Balaam as an exemplary prophetic figure. When the emissaries from Balak arrive with the king's request, Balaam consults God for direction and, when God forbids him to go, sends them away (22:7-14). When Balak entices Balaam by sending more and higher-ranking officials, and with a "name your price" offer, Balaam again refuses, this time emphatically declaring that Balak cannot pay him enough "to do anything, whether great or small, that goes beyond the direction of YHWH my God" (22:18). Balaam is thus portrayed as an individual of uncompromising integrity and a dutiful servant of YHWH, who does not act presumptuously and cannot be compromised by the temptation to gain wealth or prestige.

Yet Balaam does something that anticipates how he will later deal with Balak. After his emphatic refusal to go beyond YHWH's directive, Balaam invites the emissaries to stay for the night, saying "Let me find out if YHWH says anything more to me" (22:19). The statement echoes Balaam's response to the first group of emissaries (v. 8), but results in a different response. In the first instance, YHWH tersely commands Balaam, "You are not to go with them. You are not to curse the nation, because it is blessed" (v. 12). Yet, this time YHWH declares, "Get up. Go with them. But do only what I tell you to do" (v. 20). The instruction draws us back to what YHWH directed Balaam in the first place, and particularly the reason YHWH gave for refusing the emissaries: the Israelites are blessed. In light of YHWH's prior declaration, why did Balaam not dismiss the emissaries immediately? Why did he instead tell them to remain so that he could find out whether YHWH had anything more to say? What more need YHWH say, having already expressed his will to Balaam in unambiguous terms in the first instance? Why, in short, would Balaam seek a second consultation? And why, when he does, would YHWH tell him to go?

What transpires when Balaam departs suggests an answer to the last question. God is angered that Balaam has gone with the emissaries, and the angel of YHWH blocks his way, ready to strike him down (22:22). YHWH's anger and action, however, clash with what YHWH has directed Balaam to do. Does God's anger then issue from caprice? The end of the account lends clarity. When YHWH opens Balaam's eyes and announces that he has been spared, Balaam prostrates himself and confesses that he has sinned (v. 34). But what is his sin? That he beat the donkey and tried to push ahead? Or that he decided to go with the officials of Moab in the first place? Balaam confirms the latter by offering to go back if YHWH is displeased.

YHWH reiterates his command that Balaam accompany the men and do only what he has been told (v. 35, cf. v. 20). Now, however, that command reverberates with divine anger and displeasure. The second iteration thus nuances the first, intimating that YHWH's directive that Balaam accompany the men did not express God's will. It was rather a concession, or more likely, a test.[4] YHWH has already disclosed his disposition toward Israel in response to the first delegation (v. 12). No more need be said. Balaam's second consultation, however, signals that he thinks YHWH might be inclined to change his mind; YHWH may say something more (v. 19). In a sense, this is what YHWH does by telling Balaam to go, but now the command expresses divine displeasure rather than divine endorsement.

Balaam's consultation of YHWH in the second instance, when Balaam knows what YHWH has already spoken, signals why Balaam directs Balak to offer seven burnt offerings on seven altars, and to do so repeatedly after YHWH has given Balaam blessings to speak over Israel rather than curses (23:1-24:13). The odd and excessive repetition of sacrifice has puzzled interpreters, who generally view the sacrifices as part of the ritual process of divination.[5] This however misses the point. The whole course of the narrative thus far prepares us to view the sacrifices as attempts to change YHWH's disposition toward Israel and authorize curses instead of blessing. The sacrifices should be seen, in short, as acts of *intercession* rather than *divination*.

Recognizing the sacrificial process as intercession explains why it is extravagant. The bulls and rams sacrificed on the seven altars are offered as gifts to YHWH with the expectation that YHWH may be cajoled into changing what he has declared concerning Israel.[6] The sacrifices are lavish and excessive because YHWH has been adamant that Israel is not to be cursed; it will take a great stock of gifts to get YHWH to reconsider. By directing the sacrifices, Balaam intimates to Balak what he has implied earlier to the emissaries: although YHWH has made his will known, he might be persuaded to say something different if the dialogue is extended and sufficient gifts are offered (22:19).

In directing the sacrifices, Balaam therefore functions as a mediator for Balak. This is why, after offering the sacrifices, Balaam tells Balak to wait while he goes away to meet YHWH and receive YHWH's response (23:1-3, 15). It is why Balaam points out the lavish array of sacrifices when God meets him the first time (v. 4). And it is why Balak, who understands the capricious exactitude by which gods must be approached, looks for a more opportune spot to sacrifice after each of the first two attempts fail to produce the desired result. Balak takes a negative response as an indication that the deity wants more, just as Balak's emissaries took Balaam's initial refusal as a signal that he could be persuaded if Balak offered more (22:15-17). The intercessory process thus involves trying again, with increasing gifts and a search for just the right place to offer them.

Balaam's first two oracles confirm that the intent of the sacrifices is to change what YHWH has decreed concerning Israel. The first oracle makes clear that Balaam cannot utter a curse when God has not authorized one, yet creates a sense of openness by rendering the message as a question: "How can I curse what God does not curse? How can I denounce what YHWH won't denounce?" (23:8). The second oracle then builds indirectly on the first oracle (via questions) and responds directly to what Balaam is enticing YHWH to do: "God is not human, that he should dissemble, nor a child of Adam that he should change his mind. Would he say something and not do it? Or declare something and not fulfill it?"(23:19).

The third time around is therefore an exercise in futility. Balak wants to try again, and Balaam goes along with him (23:27-30). Balaam, however, realizes that

YHWH is determined to bless Israel and no longer bothers to find a place for a meeting (24:1). After the third set of sacrifices, God stops the process altogether and takes control of it by moving upon Balaam by the power of his spirit (24:2). The resulting oracle makes it abundantly clear that the Lord will not change what God has spoken, reinforcing the declaration by echoing the promise that God gave Abram: those who bless Israel will be blessed, but those who curse Israel will be cursed (24:9b; cf. Gen 12:3). After costly sacrificing and accruing blessing for Israel, an enraged Balak gets the point and quits (24:10-11). Balaam then confirms the futility of the enterprise. This God is faithful to do what he has said and cannot be influenced by human manipulation (24:12-13).

BALAAM AND MOSES

Neither Balaam nor Moses is a prophet. Moses is more than a prophet, and Balaam resembles one. Both however exhibit attributes that exemplify prophetic ministry. Both speak what YHWH, and only what YHWH, gives them to speak. Both manifest a tenacious steadfastness in God's service and a determination not to diverge from what God commands. Both give due deference to YHWH. And both assume the role of intercessors and attempt to change divine decrees.

Intercession, however, is where the two prophetic figures differ profoundly. Balaam undertakes his intercession in response to human bidding, specifically an attempt to curse a nation that is deemed a threat by the petitioner. Although Balaam knows what God has said and operates within divine parameters, he acts as if this deity can be persuaded to change if the right mechanism can be found. Moses, for his part, also attempts to change YHWH's mind. Yet Moses intercedes within the context of a deep relationship with YHWH, rather than by way of personal or magical power. Moses does not employ ritual or divination but issues a direct appeal for mercy when circumstances have prompted YHWH to decree destruction (Num 12:13; 14:13-19; cf. Exod 32:11-14). Most importantly, Moses knows YHWH to be a deity who is not capricious but rather is compassionate and gracious, slow to anger and full of love and faithfulness (Exod 34:6).

Taken as a whole, the Balaam narrative presents its protagonist as a prophetic anti-type to Moses and thus provides guidance for discerning the trustworthiness of prophetic figures. Prophets may speak in the name of Yhwh and display exemplary integrity and obedience. Nevertheless, the narrative suggests, their trustworthiness is to be discerned in the way that they relate to and present the God of Israel, and specifically in the way they undertake intercession. If their way with YHWH renders YHWH little different than all other deities, they are not true prophets like Moses. The Balaam narrative thus expresses "the unrelenting vigilance of the Torah in denying man any share in the manipulation of divine power" (Milgrom 1990:454).

The story of Moses at Meribah sets the contrast in sharp relief. Both this and the Balaam narrative reveal that YHWH will brook no word or interaction that is not faithful to treat him as holy, that is, truly and utterly different than all other deities. The difference in the case of Moses is that Moses' resort to a quasi-magical ritual issues from a momentary and exceptional eruption of anger, whereas Balaam's ritualistic scheme manifests an approach that views YHWH as little different from the other deities that populated ancient pantheons.

"This deity," John Oswalt writes of YHWH, "was *not* fickle, undependable, self-serving, and grasping. Instead he was faithful, true, upright, and generous — always" (Oswalt 2009:71). To borrow Oswalt's language, the Balaam narrative prompts readers to assess prophetic figures in terms of whether the practitioner manifests a sense of transcendence or continuity when relating to the God of Israel. Trustworthy prophets do not, in fact must not, use magical practices, nor attempt "to lay hold of divine power" to accomplish their purposes (2009:76). YHWH is, above all, radically other and separate from all of creation, beyond manipulation, and totally free to decide, work and fulfill as he pleases. YHWH is *holy*. His servants can be recognized therefore not so much by the gifts they display as by the way they express and honor this central truth about the God of Israel.

END NOTES

[1] Jacob Milgrom (1990:448-455) notes the affinities between Moses' striking the rock and Mesopotamian magic, where spells were cast by uttering words while making conventional gestures. In all other miracles, he argues, Moses remains silent. In this case, Moses acts presumptuously and imitates the pagan cults, which presumed that the gods were subject to occult powers.

[2] See particularly Baruch Levine, who argues that the point of contention has to do with Balaam's acknowledgement that the power to curse was subject to a deity's authorization to do so rather than resident within himself (Levine 1993:212-16). The overlapping of these functions is attested in Syro-Palestinian sources, leading to the proposal that Balaam did not want to subordinate his role as soothsayer to that of sorcerer, in opposition to Balak's wishes (Chavalas 2003:78).

[3] Jacob Milgrom (1990:472-473) considers this the major tension in the story. Balak wants Balaam to curse Israel, but Balaam can only divine for Balak. Noting that sorcerers nowhere curse the kings' enemies in Mesopotamian literature, Milgrom suggests that Balak should not have expected a resident of northern Mesopotamia to carry out that function.

[4] An early prophetic tradition reports a similar test (1 Kgs 13:1-32). In this case a man of God delivers an oracle against Jeroboam I and the altar at Bethel and refuses payment for intercession in terms reminiscent of Balaam's refusal (v. 8; cf. Num 22:18). The man of God also discloses YHWH's command that he not eat or drink, but return directly home by the way he came. An old prophet, however, entices the man to eat and drink at his house. The man initially refuses but is persuaded by the prophet's deceptive report that the angel of YHWH told him to bring the man back. As the man is eating, the prophet accuses him of disobeying what God told him in the first place and pronounces a death sentence. When the man of God leaves, a lion attacks and kills him.

[5] The conventional view is articulated by Martin Noth (1968:182), who writes that Balaam offers the sacrifices to prompt a meeting and get instructions. So also Thomas Dozeman (1998:185): "The sacrifices are part of a ritual of divination, perhaps intended to prompt God's appearance."

[6] Studies of sacrifice across cultures reveal that they are often governed by the logic of mutual exchange, a sort of *quid pro quo* (Nelson 1993:62-63). Biblical texts attest that the mentality was present among some in Israel but flatly rejects such an understanding of sacrifice (e.g. Psa 50:6-13; Mic 6:1-6).

Works Cited

Chavalas, Mark
    2003   "Balaam." Pages 75-78 in *Dictionary of the Old Testament: Pentateuch*. Edited by T. Desmond Alexander and David W. Baker. Downers Grove, IL: InterVarsity Press.

Dozeman, Thomas
    1998   "The Book of Numbers." Pages 3-311 in *The New Interpreter's Bible*. Edited by Leander Keck. Vol. 2. Nashville: Abingdon.

Lienhard, Joseph T., ed.,
    2001   *Exodus, Leviticus, Numbers, Deuteronomy*, ACCS: OT 3. 3rd ed. Downers Grove, IL: InterVarsity Press.

Levine, Baruch
    1993   *Numbers 1-20*. AB 4a. New York: Doubleday.

Milgrom, Jacob
    1990   *Numbers*. JPSTC. Philadelphia: Jewish Publication Society.

Nelson, Richard
    1993   *Raising Up a Faithful Priest*. Louisville: Westminster/John Knox.

Noth, Martin
    1968   *Numbers*. OTL. Translated by James D. Martin. Philadelphia: Westminster.

Oswalt, John N.
    2009   *The Bible among the Myths*. Grand Rapids, MI: Zondervan.

The Function of Psalmic Prayers in Chronicles: Literary-Rhetorical Method in Conversation With Ritual Theory[1]

MICHAEL D. MATLOCK

KEYWORDS:

1-2 Chronicles, 1 Chronicles 16:8-36, prayer, ritual, Psalm

Michael D. Matlock (PhD, Hebrew Union College- Jewish Institute of Religion) is Professor of Inductive Biblical Studies, Old Testament, and Early Judaism at Asbury Theological Seminary in Wilmore, Kentucky.

Abstract

The content, location, and integration of each recorded and reported prayer text in the narrative of 1-2 Chronicles largely determines the forceful rhetorical functions of prayer within the narrative contexts and helps to establish early Jewish identity in the Second Temple period. The editors of the book adapt prayers to new settings and distinct needs of the faith community. Through the discourse of psalmic prayer (1 Chr 16:8-36; 16:41; 2 Chr 5:13; 6:40-42; 7:3; 7:6; and 20:21) in relationship to elements of ritual, ideas may become embodied and appropriated by the participants of these prayers.

Introduction

Through ritual theories, researchers have made key contributions to the study of religions and of human cultures. They call attention to behaviors rather than beliefs, and especially to repeated practices shaped by social custom and religious mandate. Within societies dominated by traditional forms of monarchy, ritual activities are central to cultural life. Hence, ritual can serve as a convenient example of the forces shaping all forms of social action.[2]

By comparison, the ancient Israelites were ruled by a king for many centuries going all the way back to the days of King Saul. By the late Persian period, when the monarchy was approximately two centuries removed, the ancient Yehudites' historical and cultural memory was still dominated by an analysis of their prior kingship. The books of Chronicles preserve divine revelation, but also serve as important cultural artifacts from this period primarily by recounting and reinterpreting the divinely sanctioned Davidic kingship in ancient Israel. Through various methodological analyses of the ubiquitous ritual of prayer in these sacred books,[3] the forces shaping social action can be more clearly observed. From the perspective of several consensus concepts in ritual theory, this exploration raises questions about how such practices of psalmic prayer should be interpreted and appropriated. Although this essay is largely a theoretical discussion, my aim is to pay tribute to Professor Oswalt's unwavering desire to interpret and appropriate scripture in a manner that brings the people of God into closer relationship to the covenant God revealed in scripture.

I. Synopsis of a Previous Study of the Literary-Rhetorical Function of Prayers and Psalms in the Narrative of Chronicles

In a previous literary-rhetorical and ideological study, this author argued that the Chronicler's shaping of prayers and psalms functions in large measure to demonstrate the inclusivity of prayer for a people without a king, but not without a cult.[4] Direct and indirect prayer speech is a pervasive feature in the books of Chronicles. I observed eleven reported or indirect prayers (1 Chr 5.20; 21.26; 2 Chr 12.6; 13.14; 18.31; 20.26; 30.27; 31.8; 32.20; 32.24; 33.12-13) and nineteen recorded or direct prayers and psalms (twelve narrative prayers: 1 Chr 4.10; 14.10; 17.16-27; 21.8; 21.17; 29.10-20; 2 Chr 1.8-10; 6.3-11; 6.14-42; 14.10; 20.5-12; and 30.18-19; and seven psalmic prayers: 1 Chr 16.8-36; 16.41; 2 Chr 5.13; 6.40-42; 7:3; 7:6; and 20:21).

There are at least two larger historical frameworks located in Chronicles, namely the broader human history in the genealogical portion (1 Chr 1-9) and the specific monarchic history of Israel as a united then divided kingdom (1 Chr 10 – 2 Chr 36). Of the thirty prayers and psalms, only two appear in the larger human history; nevertheless, these two non-royal *Sondergut* prayers, Jabez's prayer (1 Chr 4.10) and the prayer of the tribes of Reuben, Gad, and half-tribe of Manasseh (1 Chr 5.20), function programmatically to maintain the efficacy of prayer to assist in the substantial physical needs (land and protection) of the late Persian period Yehudite community.

Out of the monarchic history, twenty of the twenty-eight prayers and psalms come from the mouths of Israelite kings (united/divided kingdoms). Kings David, Solomon, Jehoshaphat, and Hezekiah are the supplicants of seventeen of these twenty. Through the literary feature of characterization, the Chronicler is able to present striking profiles of a kingly character's moral and religious disposition to help the intended readers understand, evaluate, and react to these kings. In my previous research, I reaffirmed that royal figures are characterized by one of three manners: largely or totally negative representation, negative and positive portrayal, and largely or totally positive depiction.[5]

Of the twenty royal prayers, fourteen prayers come from kings characterized in a largely positive manner and the other six prayers stem from kings characterized as a mixture of negative and positive features. No prayers arise from the kings who are portrayed in a primarily negative manner. Of the kings depicted with a mixture of negative and positive features, Manasseh's reported prayer is part of a characterization that demonstrates remarkable repentance and the rare exception of a "bad-turned-good" king. Solomon's four prayers, which include one psalm, are part of an idealized characterization of the king (as opposed to the realistic one in the Deuteronomistic History). Solomon is presented as a royal paragon in terms of morals, politics, and the cult. Moreover, Solomon's prayers and psalm concerning the dedication of the temple are utilized for the pattern of anticipation and recollection for other royal prayers offered in the book of Chronicles.

In the final section of the research, I focused on the literary-rhetorical function of the *Sondergut* prayers and psalms. One very prominent feature of these prayers is that the royal supplicants exhibit piety in crisis and demonstrate a marked contrast between futile human weakness (from a king, no less) and the potency of divine strength. As for the seven *Sondergut* psalms in Chronicles, the Chronicler has added to the notion of speaking prayers by recounting the dramatic effect of singing prayers. Six of the seven psalms are prayed by non-royal figures. Regarding the rhetorical function of singing a prayer, I concluded that music almost always plays an important role in all mass movements, because it ties the people together and submerges the individual (cf. the distain for the use of music in a mass movement from the biblical writer of Daniel 3). Prayer that is sung or chanted will sustain prayer much longer than prayer divorced from music.

One can observe a significant irony in the corpus of prayers regarding the situation of the late Persian Yehudite readers. While the royal prayers are dominant and catch the reader's main focus on a first reading, it is the non-royal prayers and the bridge prayers (royal and non-royal together) that pave the way to a brighter, more contextually appropriate relationship with YHWH. Moreover, the Chronicler introduces the seven psalmic prayers to broaden the application and necessity of prayer for the late Persian-period Yehudite community, which is dominated by the centrality of the cult without a king in order to restore hope and as a means to receive YHWH's favor.

II. Distinguishing Between Texts and Rituals

Here I compare and distinguish the nature of a literary-rhetorical lens for prayer texts and a type of ritual studies interpretive lens. Greenberg makes two salient points in his little treatise, *Biblical Prose Prayer as a Window to the Popular Religion of Ancient Israel*. First, Greenburg makes the important case for studying prayer by social analogy to the manner of interhuman discourse and speech patterns.[6] Prayer, which is a human-divine communication, functions much the same way human-human communication works. Thus, he denotes how inferiors speak to superiors in terms of address, confession, gratitude, forms, as well as patterns of interhuman speech and conventions expressing such things as greetings, leave-takings, politeness, hortatory addresses, traditional articulations in set situations, dependence, subjection, and obligation.

When it comes to understanding ritual, although not unique to it, Wright argues a similar point in that theological constructs often arise out of "anthropo-metaphorical" contexts.[7] Divine-human analogies such as redeemer, savior, father, and king all arise from human institutions, namely the economy, the military, the family, and the monarchy. One of the reasons rituals are performed is because of "analogy's power to advance conceptualization," making it possible to "conceive of, discuss, and develop hitherto unexpressed ideas.[8] Moreover, Wright states that analogies "give participants some control—at least psychological control—over something that is threatening or elusive. This alone may be sufficient reason to perform a rite, even if the desired outcome does not have a history or likelihood of being fulfilled."[9] Even though Wright's comments are intended for the ritual of sacrifice in the Hebrew Bible, his suggestions are justly transferable to the ritual of prayer. Thus, I have altered his quote regarding biblical sacrifice involving analogy to the ritual of prayer: "just as a human lord is honored, praised, entreated, or appeased through [speech], so the divine Lord is honored, praised, entreated, or appeased through [speech termed prayer]."[10]

Greenburg's second salient point is that when understanding the nature and function of narrative prayer, there is a continuum of extemporaneous prayer on one side of the spectrum and ritual, prescribed prayer on the other side. Throughout the continuum, Greenberg argues that all levels of patterned prayer speech are composed with language, style and phraseology.[11] Although Greenberg did not explicitly make this point, his insight into the spectrum of prayer undergirds a touchstone that Wuthnow, Bell, and other ritual theorists have brought to the fore. Ritual and non-ritual activity should not be viewed with a strict dichotomous lens.[12]

Ritual is not a special dimension of social activity but rather a dimension of all social activity. Wuthnow concludes, "Ritual is not a type of social activity that can be set off from the rest of the world for special investigation. It is a dimension of all social activity. The study of ritual, therefore, is not distinguished by its concern with certain types of activity, but by the perspective it brings to bear on all activity, namely, emphasis on the symbolic or expressive dimension of behavior."[13] Rappaport argues that ritual is on a continuum of formality found in all behavior and denotes "ritual" in the singular as referring to the formal aspect of all behavior, and "rituals" in the plural as indicating unchanging events completely dominated by formality.[14]

One can find another area of commonality between the interpretation of texts and rituals in elements utilized for interpretation of either phenomena. Formal properties noted in both interpretations are repetition and other literary structural devices such as chiasms, syntax, order and sequence, geographical and temporal referents, action and objects of action, participants, and sound referents.[15] Thus, for example in the interpretation of texts, Freedman insists that one of the major emphases of recent literary investigation is the attempt "to discern clusters or families of related words or phrases that, by virtue of their frequency and particular use, tell us something about the author's intentions, conscious or otherwise."[16] And regarding repetition in ritual, the formal repetitive character of ritual leads to continuity in which the major accent falls, as well as some discontinuity in which the minor accent falls.

Whereas the first three points indicate continuities between interpretation of texts and ritual, this last point denotes a distinction in that texts may reflect interests and meanings different from the rituals they describe.[17] Gilders has cautioned that both the ritual and the text need an interpretation and thus the interpreter of ritual and text must

> "distinguish carefully between the "world of the text" and a living, historical context in which ritual activity takes place. The latter context is not immediately accessible to the reader of the Bible. Only after we have developed a clear picture of the world of the text can we attempt to reconstruct an image of the real world in which ritual actions might have been carried out."[18]

It seems prudent thus to offer a working definition of ritual at this junction. Because Bell's contours offer the most promise for my investigation, I define ritual as action that distinguishes itself from other ways of acting in the very way it does what it does.[19] Ritual is constructed out of widely accepted blocks of tradition and generates a sense of cultural continuity even when the juxtaposition of these blocks defines a unique ritual ethos.[20] In terms of socialization, ritual practice results in a ritualized body or "cultivated disposition."[21]

III. RITUALIZATION IN THE PSALMIC PRAYERS IN CHRONICLES

A. Interpreting Psalmic Prayer Texts

As noted above, there are seven poetic, psalmic prayers found in Chronicles (1 Chr 16:8-36; 16:41; 2 Chr 5:13; 6:40-42; 7:3; 7:6; and 20:21). Within the first and by far the lengthiest psalm, 1 Chr 16:8-36, King David asks Asaph, one of the prominent leaders of the temple singers and musician guilds, to lead the Israelites in singing and praying the psalm. This psalmic prayer is the only extensive poetry in Chronicles. The prayer includes the bracketed command to give thanks to YHWH and the confession that YHWH is good and his *hesed* is eternal; thus, it sets the rhetorical stage for the purpose of praying a psalm.

The psalm consists of portions of three psalms: Pss 105:1-15; 96:1-13; and 106:1, 47-48. Beyond any doubt, the Chronicler, with the benefit of these psalms, has created a totally new context of his own.[22] The new psalm in 1 Chr 16:8-36 contains thirty-one imperatival forms (imperatives and jussives) addressing the reader.[23] The three main units of the psalm are as follows: 1) defining what it means to praise the Lord and rationale (vv. 8-22); 2) a call to praise YHWH over all the nations, and therefore over their gods and the whole earth (vv. 23-33); and 3) a summon to YHWH's people as a whole to join the Levites' praise (vv. 34-36).

David's appointed psalm that Asaph and his musical group are to sing and pray in worship contains a heightened importance for the worship of YHWH. Asaph's psalm is to be sung *to the LORD* (v. 4) before the ark of God's covenant, which has now been brought into the center of Israel's life. These elements serve as the setting (vv. 4-6, 37) and provide the primary purpose of the psalm. The first main unit of Asaph's psalm gives definition to what it means to praise the Lord (vv. 8-13; cf. Ps 105:1-6), and the rationale to do so, namely because of his faithfulness to the Abrahamic covenant (vv. 14-18; cf. Ps 105:7-11). It is a covenant of YHWH's unmerited favor and love that he demonstrates although undeserved by choosing and rescuing his people when they were unable to help themselves (vv. 19-22; cf. Ps 105:12-15).

The second unit of the psalm commands international and cosmic praise for YHWH as God over all the nations and their gods,[24] and indeed over the whole earth (vv. 23-33; cf. Ps 96:1-13). The final unit of Asaph's psalm contains a summons for the entirety of God's people to unite with the Levites' praise (vv. 34-36; cf. Ps 106:1, 47-48). The imperative to give thanks to YHWH, which commences the psalm, is repeated again in v. 34 forming an inclusio to strength the programmatic action. Within this climactic section of the psalm, the main reason to offer thanks is revealed: YHWH's unwavering love continues for a very long duration (kî lə'ôlām ḥasdô). The Israelites are instructed to pray to their God of salvation by praying "save us" (hôšî'ēnû) and "rescue us" (haṣṣîlēnû) from the nations so that they are in a better position to give thanks to YHWH's holy name (35).

The other six psalmic prayers in Chronicles all contain some version of 1 Chr 16:34, "Give thanks to YHWH, for he is good; for his steadfast love is eternal." Like this verse, each one of the six are offered by non-royal figures (singers, Levites, all Israel) and refer to the Lord in third person in the prayer, except for the psalmic prayer that Solomon prays at the end of his temple dedication prayer in which the Lord is addressed in second person (2 Chr 6:42). In a way, these other six prayers are riffing off of this long programmatic psalm, specifically 1 Chr 16:34.

Many interpreters have argued that the words in Exod 34:6-7 became Israel's clearest and most ancient confession, and they may be regarded as a foundational theological statement of scripture, out of which everything else flows. Thus, 1 Chr 16:34 may be viewed as one of many articulations of this ancient confession. Miller avers that this expression is "as close as one can come to an ancient creed or to the Hebrew Bible answer to the catechism question: 'What is God?'"[25]

So, why does the Chronicler include the psalmic prayers, none of which are found in the Deuteronomistic History? If the non-psalmic prayers proclaim, "YHWH, you are our God,"[26] then the psalmic prayers proclaim the same but with the caveat that it is right to give thanks to YHWH because he is good and his *hesed* endures forever. Moreover, to the rhetorical elements of speaking prayer, the Chronicler adds the dramatic effect of singing prayer. Whereas kings dominate in terms of those who offer prayers, non-royalty personsb dominate in offering psalms in Chronicles. More precisely, worship personnel containing priests and Levites chiefly offer psalm speech. This emphasis on psalmic prayer strengthens another main theme of the Chronicler, the reimposition of temple personnel and employment.

Interestingly, four of the seven occurrences appear in the section where Solomon dedicates the temple (2 Chr 5:2-7:11) and one of these four is the only psalm offered by royalty, namely Solomon (6:40-42). Unlike in Solomon's dedicatory prayer in 1 Kings 8, the Chronicler reports that Solomon ends his long narrative prayer with a psalm. His ending song parallels a portion of one of the Songs of Ascent, Psalm 132. In this particular psalm, the proper resting place of the ark of the covenant, namely the temple, and the continuation of David's royal line are paired in the petition.[27] The Chronicler has captured these two themes well in three verses (vv. 8-10) from Ps 132 and thus bolstered his larger rhetorical plan to promote these two themes.

B. Interpreting Ritual Arising Out of Psalmic Prayer Texts

In some societies, particularly those dominated by traditional forms of *kingship* (such as ancient Israel), ritual activities appear central to cultural life. Hence, ritual can serve as a convenient example of the forces shaping all forms of social action.[28] Thus, through the ritual of prayer, we seek to open a window into the thinking and praxis of some of the post-exilic Jewish communities. We want to unpack this "gift that lubricates the wheels of divine-human interaction."[29]

Watts notes that in antiquity, rituals do not seem to have required interpretation unless and until they were contested.[30] An interpretation of ritual is always an interpretation of interpretations. A beloved, idealized king who is praying for God's eternal favor for his people to be demonstrated, as well as Levites, temple singers and musicians, and all manner of Israelites who are making supplication to and thanking YHWH because he is good and his *hesed* is eternal, seems to give the participants of the ritual a psychological control even if recent history seems otherwise or now less likely.[31]

There certainly existed many contestations to this type of prayer ritual that focused upon thanking YHWH through prayer, which is substantiated by YHWH's eternal covenant love. Many of the approximately seventy laments in the Psalter are protesting this type of prayer ritual (e.g. Ps 22:1; 77:11 "And I say, 'It is my grief that the right hand of the Most High has changed.'" NRSV).[32] Certainly the lament text par excellence, the book of Lamentations sounds a loud voice of protest to this type of ritualization, but I hasten to add that the temple has reemerged by the late Persian period. And every one of the lament psalms except Psalm 88 concludes with a prayer of thanksgiving. At times, life was brutal and irrational. The ancient Yehudites had watched their world collapse and were pulled down into what seemed like a dark pit.

The ritualization also involved instrumental and vocal music. Music affects ritualization of prayer in numerous ways. Unfortunately, musical instruments mentioned in the Hebrew Bible are among the most perplexing phenomena of the past because insufficient "technical information about the specific nature of the employed instrument or the sound or melody that had to be produced" exists.[33] Oft times, the study of music's social context such as the sacred service may help to understand the ritualization involved. But, in the ritual of offering thanks for YHWH's goodness and eternal *hesed*, the details of the sacred service are sketchy for analysis. As noted in the rhetorical function of singing a prayer, music always plays an important role in all mass movements, because it ties the people together and submerges the individual. Prayer that is sung or chanted will sustain lasting prayer much longer than prayer without music. We might call this "praying through to praise" much like the canonical Psalter comes to a conclusion.

In terms of ritual legitimation, rather than affirming clear and dogmatic values to impress them directly into the minds of participants, ritual actually constructs an argument, a set of tensions.[34] As the Yehudites living in the late Persian period grappled with weighty issues such as the absence of the ark of the covenant, the absence of monarchy, and the lackluster temple, this prayer ritual constructed a set of tensions for reflection.

C. The Production of a Ritualized Body and Ideology

People do not simply acquire beliefs or attitudes imposed on them by others contrary to a relatively determined philosophical viewpoint. Rather, the ideology of the ritual found in the prayer speech "give thanks to YHWH for he is good and his steadfast love is eternal" is the manipulation of bias with a *clearly articulated disposition*.[35] In such cases, Bell says, "people have culturally basic 'epistemic principles' with which to evaluate and reflect upon ideas. When they agree, they do not passively follow or obey; they appropriate, negotiate, qualify."[36] The post-exilic Psalm 136, the so-called "Great Hallel" Psalm, gives the longest attestation of this psalmic prayer ritual. Clearly, part of the purpose of the twenty-six repetitions of the refrain is to allow a deepening evaluation and reflection upon this ritual action. McCann asserts, "the psalmist affirms that every aspect and moment of Israel's story... is pervaded by and dependent upon God's steadfast love."[37]

Ideology has less to do with a state of mind and more to do with a set of practices that prevent the potentially infinite meaning of various cultural elements and relations in determinate ways. Following Bell, the implications are such that our understanding of the actor-subject-agent of the ritual who is both embedded in and generative of ideology is affected.[38] The actor emerges as a divided, decentered, overly determined, but quite active subject. Bourdieu's concept of how an agent develops through habitus may also help us conceptualize how the ideology of the ritual in this psalmic prayer may be operative in the reader. Bourdieu argues that an actor is constituted by structured and structuring dispositions.[39] In other words, through repeated results from an organizing principle, a predisposition, tendency, propensity, or inclination develops in a person.

There are also important parallel developments from cognitive science, such as McNamara's research studies in self-development and religious experience from the vantage point of neuroscience.[40] Simply stated, McNamara's central contention is that the brain helps shape expression of both religion and Self (a person's identity), arguing that the Self begins fragmentary and then decenters to achieve defragmentation and promote healing. In order to achieve the ideal Self, one must receive help from God. God's assistance can produce a new and improved Self but it "is an arduous process that requires years of effort."[41] Furthermore, ritual, such as prayer, serves to decenter a person's identity and yoke that person with the identity of God by bringing into focus God's presence. A standardized or "canonical message" such as 1 Chr 16:34 delivered as ritual prayer speech encourages readers/listeners "to identify with those messages, to speak them and to internalize them" and "form a bond with the deity."[42] What does this mean for ancient Yehudites engaged in the ritualization of this brand of psalmic prayer? The ancient Yehudite engaged in this psalmic prayer ritual had an opportunity to move on the spectrum of fragmented personhood (Self) by embracing the realities of the prayer at various degrees of "defragmentation" and choose to move into a more intimate relationship with YHWH, propelled by a deeper religious experience of his covenant love and goodness.

Finally, Bell reminds us that "it may well be the constraints of community as much as the interests of particular groups that hold ideas together for the sake of flexibly unformulated, but practically coherent, worldview, even when that worldview limits, ranks, marginalizes, or frustrates."[43] In terms of the ancient Yehudite engaged in this ritual psalmic prayer, we must acknowledge that the established order produced by the Yehudite scribal ranks who promoted the ritual in textual form also promoted a coherent worldview that the divine was benevolent to his covenant people. Certainly, this ritualization would have brought a certain level of frustration to the agent of the ritual due to the failure of the monarchy and the shortcoming of the larger cult.

Conclusion

I conclude not with a conclusion or summary, but rather with an observation. After this rather brief comparison of the difference between the interpretation of a prayer text and the interpretation of prayer ritual, I more clearly understand why Watts indicates his disapproval of some of Milgrom's treatment of ritual texts in P on the one hand, and Douglas's analysis on the other hand.[44] Milgrom was a distinguished biblical scholar, and Douglas an accomplished anthropologist. But, both scholars were not consistent in critically observing the differences between texts and rituals. The collapse can be very subtle if a researcher is not keenly aware of the different methods that ought to be used to interpret text and ritual.

END NOTES

[1] An earlier version of this essay was presented in the Prayer in Antiquity Consultation at the Annual Meeting of the SBL, Atlanta, GA, 24 November 2015.

[2] Catherine M. Bell, *Ritual: Perspectives and Dimensions* (Oxford: Oxford University Press, 2009), 77. See Jacob Milgrom's three-volume magisterial commentary on Leviticus, *Leviticus 1-16*; *Leviticus 17-22*; *Leviticus 23-27*, The Anchor Bible (New York: Doubleday, 1991; 2000; 2001) for a sustained discussion of ritual studies and ritual impact in the book.

[3] Samuel E. Balentine, "'You Can't Pray a Lie': Truth and Fiction in the Prayers of Chronicles," in *Chronicler as Historian*, ed. M. Patrick Graham, Kenneth Hoglund, and Steven McKenzie (Sheffield: Sheffield Academic, 1997), 246–67; Pancratius C. Beentjes, "'Give Thanks to YHWH. Truly He Is Good': Psalms and Prayers in the Book of Chronicles," in *Tradition and Transformation in the Book of Chronicles*, Studia Semitica Neerlandica 52 (Leiden: Brill, 2008), 141–43.

[4] Michael D. Matlock, "Rhetorically and Ideologically Shaping the Narrative Through Direct and Indirect Prayer Speech in Chronicles," in *Prayers: Remembering and Constructing Israelite Identity*, ed. Susanne Gillmayr-Bucher, SBL: Ancient Israel and Its Literature (Atlanta: SBL Press, forthcoming).

[5] Richard Pratt, "First and Second Chronicles," in *A Complete Literary Guide to the Bible*, ed. Leland Ryken and Tremper Longman (Grand Rapids: Zondervan, 1993), 194–95.

[6] Moshe Greenberg, *Biblical Prose Prayer as a Window to the Popular Religion of Ancient Israel*, Taubman Lectures in Jewish Studies (Berkeley: Univ of California Press, 1983), 19–37.

[7] David P. Wright, "The Study of Ritual in the Hebrew Bible," in *The Hebrew Bible: New Insights and Scholarship*, ed. Frederick E. Greenspahn, Jewish Studies in the 21st Century (New York: NYU Press, 2008), 128–34.

[8] Ibid., 129.

[9] Ibid.

[10] Ibid., 130.

[11] Greenberg, *Biblical Prose Prayer as a Window to the Popular Religion of Ancient Israel*, 44–46.

[12] Wright, "The Study of Ritual in the Hebrew Bible," 121; Catherine M. Bell, *Ritual Theory, Ritual Practice* (New York: Oxford University Press, 2009), 69–93.

[13] Robert Wuthnow, *Meaning and Moral Order: Explorations in Cultural Analysis* (Berkeley: University of California Press, 1989), 121.

[14] Roy A. Rappaport, *Ecology, Meaning, and Religion* (Richmond, CA: North Atlantic Books, 1979), 174–78.

[15] See Gerald A. Klingbeil, *Bridging the Gap: Ritual and Ritual Texts in the Bible*, Bulletin for Biblical Research Supplements (Winona Lake, IN: Eisenbrauns, 2007), 147–204; Sally Moore and Barbara Myerhoff, "Secular Ritual: Forms and Meanings," in *Secular Ritual*, ed. Sally Moore and Barbara Myerhoff (Assen, Netherlands: Van Gorcum, 1977), 7–8.

[16] William Freedman, "The Literary Motif: A Definition and Evaluation," *NOVEL: A Forum on Fiction* 4.2 (1971): 123.

[17] James W. Watts, *Ritual and Rhetoric in Leviticus: From Sacrifice to Scripture* (Cambridge University Press, 2007), 1–36.

[18] William K. Gilders, *Blood Ritual in the Hebrew Bible: Meaning and Power* (Baltimore: The Johns Hopkins University Press, 2004), 11.

[19] See Bell, *Ritual*, 81.

[20] See Bell, *Ritual Theory, Ritual Practice*, 195.

[21] See ibid., 98–101; Pierre Bourdieu, *Outline of a Theory of Practice*, Cambridge Studies in Social Anthropology (Cambridge: Cambridge University Press, 1977), 87–93, 118–20, 124.

[22] Beentjes, "'Give Thanks to YHWH. Truly He Is Good': Psalms and Prayers in the Book of Chronicles," 169; Mark A. Throntveit, "Songs in a New Key: The Psalmic Structure of the Chronicler's Hymn (1 Chr 16:8-36)," in *A God So Near* (Winona Lake, IN: Eisenbrauns, 2003), 153–54; Louis C. Jonker, "The Chronicler Singing Psalms: Revisiting the Chronicler's Psalm in 1 Chronicles 16," in *"My Spirit at Rest in the North Country" (Zechariah 6.8)* (Frankfurt am Main: Peter Lang, 2011), 115–16.

[23] Beentjes, "'Give Thanks to YHWH. Truly He Is Good': Psalms and Prayers in the Book of Chronicles," 171. Imperatives are found in the following verses: 8 (3x), 9 (3x), 10, 11 (2x), 12, 15, 23 (2x), 24, 28 (2x), 29 (4x), 30, 34, and 35 (4x); jussives are located in vv. 10, 31 (2x), and 32 (2x).

[24] See 1 Chr 14:12 for an initial international abandonment of false gods.

[25] Patrick D. Miller, *The Lord of the Psalms* (Louisville: Westminster John Knox, 2013), 75.

[26] Samuel E. Balentine, *Prayer In The Hebrew Bible, The Drama of Divine Human Dialogue*, OBT (Minneapolis: Fortress, 1993), 102.

[27] As noted by Ralph Klein ("Psalms in Chronicles," *Currents in Theology and Mission* 32.4 [2005]: 272), the Chronicler's allotment and placement of Psalm 132 downplays the concept of dynastic rule by placing it last and elevates the importance of temple and people.

[28] Bell, *Ritual*, 77.

[29] Wright, "The Study of Ritual in the Hebrew Bible," 125.

[30] Watts, *Ritual and Rhetoric in Leviticus*, 34.

[31] Cf. Wright, "The Study of Ritual in the Hebrew Bible," 129.

[32] The late title of Psalm 77 links the lament psalmic prayer to Asaph.

[33] Klingbeil, *Bridging the Gap*, 204.

[34] Bell, *Ritual Theory, Ritual Practice*, 195.

[35] Ibid., 191 as opposed to when the manipulation of bias is a matter of an unarticulated disposition such as "Stand up straight!"

[36] Ibid., 191.

[37] J. Clinton McCann, "The Book of Psalms," ed. Leander E. Keck, vol. 4, The New Interpreter's Bible (Nashville: Abingdon, 1996), 1224.

[38] Bell, *Ritual Theory, Ritual Practice*, 191–92.

[39] Bourdieu, *Outline of a Theory of Practice*, 72.

[40] Patrick McNamara, *The Neuroscience of Religious Experience* (Cambridge: Cambridge University Press, 2009) (note "fragmented Self," pp. 21-43; "decentered Self," pp. 5-6, 44-58; "ideal Self," pp. 24-26, 41-42).

[41] Ibid., 254; according McNamara, the Self is an agent that in addition to developing narratives, causes certain actions and makes decisions.

[42] Ibid., 220.

[43] Bell, *Ritual Theory, Ritual Practice*, 192.

[44] Watts, *Ritual and Rhetoric in Leviticus*, 1–36.

WORKS CITED

Balentine, Samuel E.
   1997   "'You Can't Pray a Lie': Truth and Fiction in the Prayers of Chronicles." Pages 246–67 in *Chronicler as Historian*. Edited by M. Patrick Graham, Kenneth Hoglund, and Steven McKenzie. Sheffield: Sheffield Academic.

   1993   *Prayer In The Hebrew Bible, The Drama of Divine Human Dialogue*. OBT. Minneapolis: Fortress.

Beentjes, Pancratius C.
   2008   "'Give Thanks to Yhwh. Truly He Is Good': Psalms and Prayers in the Book of Chronicles." Pages 141–76 in *Tradition and Transformation in the Book of Chronicles*. Studia Semitica Neerlandica 52. Leiden: Brill.

Bell, Catherine M.
   2009a   *Ritual: Perspectives and Dimensions*. Oxford: Oxford University Press.

   2009b   *Ritual Theory, Ritual Practice*. New York: Oxford University Press.

Bourdieu, Pierre
   1977   *Outline of a Theory of Practice*. Cambridge Studies in Social Anthropology. Cambridge: Cambridge University Press.

Freedman, William
   1971   "The Literary Motif: A Definition and Evaluation." *NOVEL: A Forum on Fiction* 4(2): 123–31.

Gilders, William K.
   2004   *Blood Ritual in the Hebrew Bible: Meaning and Power*. Baltimore: The Johns Hopkins University Press.

Greenberg, Moshe
1983 *Biblical Prose Prayer as a Window to the Popular Religion of Ancient Israel.* Taubman Lectures in Jewish Studies. Berkeley: Univ of California Press.

Jonker, Louis C.
2011 "The Chronicler Singing Psalms: Revisiting the Chronicler's Psalm in 1 Chronicles 16." Pages 115–30 in *"My Spirit at Rest in the North country" (Zechariah 6.8).* Frankfurt am Main: Peter Lang.

Klein, Ralph W.
2005 "Psalms in Chronicles." *Currents in Theology and Mission* 32(4): 264–75.

Klingbeil, Gerald A.
2007 *Bridging the Gap: Ritual and Ritual Texts in the Bible.* Bulletin for Biblical Research Supplements. Winona Lake, IN: Eisenbrauns.

Matlock, Michael D.
Forthcoming "Rhetorically and Ideologically Shaping the Narrative Through Direct and Indirect Prayer Speech in Chronicles." *Prayers: Remembering and Constructing Israelite Identity.* Edited by Susanne Gillmayr-Bucher. SBL: Ancient Israel and Its Literature. Atlanta: SBL Press.

McCann, J. Clinton
1996 "The Book of Psalms." Pages 639–1280 in . Edited by Leander E. Keck. Vol. 4. The New Interpreter's Bible. Nashville: Abingdon.

McNamara, Patrick
2009 *The Neuroscience of Religious Experience.* Cambridge: Cambridge University Press.

Milgrom, Jacob
    1991   *Leviticus 1-16: A New Translation with Introduction and Commentary*. Vol. 1. The Anchor Bible. New York: Doubleday.

Miller, Patrick D.
    2013   *The Lord of the Psalms*. Louisville: Westminster John Knox.

Moore, Sally, and Barbara Myerhoff
    1977   "Secular Ritual: Forms and Meanings." *Secular Ritual*. Edited by Sally Moore and Barbara Myerhoff. Assen, Netherlands: Van Gorcum.

Pratt, Richard
    1993   "First and Second Chronicles." Pages 193–205 in *A Complete Literary Guide to the Bible*. Edited by Leland Ryken and Tremper Longman. Grand Rapids: Zondervan.

Rappaport, Roy A.
    1979   *Ecology, Meaning, and Religion*. Richmond, CA: North Atlantic Books.

Throntveit, Mark A.
    2003   "Songs in a New Key: The Psalmic Structure of the Chronicler's Hymn (1 Chr 16:8-36)." Pages 153–70 in *A God So Near*. Winona Lake, IN: Eisenbrauns.

Watts, James W.
    2007   *Ritual and Rhetoric in Leviticus: From Sacrifice to Scripture*. Cambridge University Press.

Wright, David P.
    2008   "The Study of Ritual in the Hebrew Bible." Pages 120–39 in *The Hebrew Bible: New Insights and Scholarship*. Edited by Frederick E. Greenspahn. Jewish Studies in the 21st Century. New York: NYU Press.

Wuthnow, Robert
    1989 *Meaning and Moral Order: Explorations in Cultural Analysis.*
           Berkeley: University of California Press.

The Song of the Sea and the Subversion of Canaanite Myth: A Missional Reading

BRIAN D. RUSSELL

KEYWORDS:

Baal, missional hermeneutic, Song of the Sea, myth

Brian D. Russell (PhD, Union Theological Seminary-Presbyterian School of Christian Education) is the Dean of the School of Urban Ministries and Professor of Biblical Studies at Asbury Theological Seminary's Florida Dunnam Campus in Orlando, Florida.

Abstract

By means of explicit links to the Ugaritic Baal Cycle (*CAT* 1.1–1.6), the Song of the Sea (Exodus 15:1b–18) models missional engagement with the late Bronze/ early Iron Age cultures in which Israel emerged, and in the process enhances Israel's presentation of YHWH as the true King of the cosmos. By subverting the mythic worldview of the Baal Cycle, the Song implants a new view of creation and reality into God's people while serving as a witness to the nations of a different type of God.

Introduction

A missional hermeneutic reads scripture through the lens of mission as the interpretive key to unlocking meaning (Russell 2010). The aim of this essay is to explore how Israel's celebration of YHWH's victory at the Sea in the poetry of Exodus 15:1b–18 models a missional engagement with the late Bronze/early Iron Age culture and enhances Israel's presentation of the LORD as king of the cosmos (Hunsberger 2016:59–62). Exodus 15:1b–18 shares its structure and language in common with the Canaanite Baal Epic. Although Exodus 15:1b–18 is not myth, its allusions to Canaanite mythic themes and deployment of the broad structure of Baal's story allow Israel's proclamation of YHWH's victory over the powers of Egypt to subvert Canaanite myth and offer an alternative worldview (Russell 2016:135–136). This cultural engagement is critical for gaining insights into how to reach twenty-first century persons with the Gospel. In the ancient world just as now, conversion was never a matter of merely hearing new facts or truths. To convert fully to YHWH involved a subversion of one worldview and the implantation of a new one.

John Oswalt's *The Bible among the Myths: Unique Revelation or Just Ancient Literature* serves as a mature expression of his core conviction about the uniqueness of Israel's scripture when compared with the literature of the ancient Near East. According to Oswalt, Israel's portrayal of YHWH and its understanding of reality cannot be explained by evolutionary thinking. Oswalt has consistently followed the approach associated most prominently with William F. Albright (1969) and his student G. E. Wright (1950). Recent scholarship (e.g., Smith 2001), including an Evangelical voice (Enns 2005:23–70), has argued more for the continuity of the Old Testament with its context and seeks to explain the distinctive Israelite understanding of God and the world through an evolutionary understanding without recourse to revelation from a transcendent God.

In this essay, I want to explore the close links between Israel's literature and the mythic lore of Israel's neighbors. As Oswalt observes (2009: 12), there has been no new textual evidence unearthed to explain the pendulum swing in scholarship noted above. Oswalt views the clear differences between Israel's literature and its Canaanite counterparts as evidence for special revelation. Others explain the differences simply as Israel's unique understanding, but one that ultimately emerged over time through ordinary human reflection. Is there any way through this impasse? I argue here that through a missional reading of the Bible, the allusions to and appropriations of mythic literature can enhance our understanding of special revelation by demonstrating that it models an incarnational or missional approach to the peoples of the ancient world. Rather than demonstrating the lack of uniqueness of the Bible because of its continuity with Near Eastern literature, the close ties actually are the means by which scripture's special revelation connects cogently to its audience to subvert the Canaanite worldview for both Israelites and Canaanites who may encounter Israel's story (Currid 2013:131–141).[1] This leads to the possibility of true conversion from a pagan worldview to a biblical one in the service of God's mission to bless the nations through the people of God (Gen 12:3b; Exodus 19:4–6).

The Song of the Sea (Exod 15:1b–18) will serve as a test case for this thesis. The Song of the Sea is potentially one of the earliest extant examples of Israelite literature (Cross and Freedman 1955:237–250; Russell 2007:57–148). Moreover it testifies about Israel's core experiences of God's salvation: the victory at the Sea as the culmination of the Exodus and guidance to YHWH's holy abode.

Cross and Freedman reckoned Exodus 15:1b–18 as a "sort of 'national anthem'" in the early cult of ancient Israel (Cross and Freedman 1955:237n.f). They do not expand on this remark, but it remains suggestive. In the modern world, a national anthem serves to instill and celebrate an ethos and identity for a nation's people at public events *and* offers a testimony to other nations about the distinctive nature of the land. How does Exodus 15:1b–18 serve this role?

In the book of Exodus, the narrative testimony of the Passover and YHWH's victory at the Sea (Exod 12:1–14:31) prepares the reader for the dynamic celebration of deliverance that occurs post-deliverance on the shores of the sea. YHWH has won a great victory over the enemy of God's people. Of course, in Exodus, this enemy is the *historical* Egyptians, but the celebration is bigger than merely a one-time event. This is a victory for all times and all places. The poetry of Exodus 15:1b–18 achieves this transcendent meaning through its intentional deployment of mythic themes that it shares in common with the Baal Cycle. The Song of the Sea assumes the deliverance from the Egyptians and guidance to YHWH's holy mountain. YHWH has acted. God's people respond with a song of victory.

But we are getting ahead of ourselves. Let us first engage the spirituality and worldview of Canaan.

The Gospel According to Baal

The excavations at the ancient port city of Ugarit yielded a significant number of texts (Smith 2016:139–167). This collection of economic and religious writings serves to provide modern readers with a substantive overview of the cultural milieu of Canaan around the shift from the late Bronze to early Iron Age. The fall of Ugarit at the transition between these eras allows scholars to date these texts to the general time of Israel's emergence further to the south.

Most prominently among the Ugaritic literature is the Baal Cycle (Smith 1997: 81–176).[2] These texts tell the story of Baal's attainment of divine kingship. For those unfamiliar with the contours of Baal's tale, here is a brief summary:

In the Canaanite pantheon, El is the chief god. El is the creator and wise benefactor of creation. He reigns along with his wife Asherah. In the opening scene (*CAT* 1.1), El has decreed that Yamm (god of the Sea/River) will rule over the second tier of gods who control nature and the cycles of life and death on earth. The conflict of the Baal Cycle stems from El's decision to elevate Yamm as divine regent. This decision threatens the world as Yamm represents the power of chaos and destruction. As the personified Sea and River[3] and embodiment of the power of watery chaos, Yamm continually threatened the order of the cosmos. The elevation of Yamm constituted a direct threat to the Storm god Baal. Baal was the giver of the rains that brought life and good to the world.

In response, Baal and Yamm engage in an epic duel for supremacy (*CAT* 1.2). Baal, however, has an edge through the intervention of the divine craftsman Kothar Wa-Hasis. Kothar fashions weapons for Baal that allow him to defeat Yamm in a decisive battle. At the climax of this encounter, Baal strikes Yamm dead and destroys his body. The scene ends with the acclamation "Baal reigns" (*CAT* 1.2 IV 34–36).[4] Baal's actions are not universally lauded and the goddess Astarte rebukes him for vanquishing Yamm.

To celebrate Baal's position of supremacy over the gods he enjoys a feast complete with a huge goblet of alcohol and a collection of female deities (*CAT* 1.3). At this point, the warrior goddess Anat enters and the Baal Cycle narrates a bloody sequence in which Anat slaughters human warriors mercilessly. This is the sole appearance of humans within the Baal Cycle.

Baal's rule is enhanced by the building of a palace for him on the holy mountain of Zaphan (*CAT* 1.4). Kothar Wa-Hasis is again present to aid in the construction. Upon its completion, there is a banquet held in which Baal entertains other gods and goddesses. In the final columns of *CAT* 1.4, the tensions between Baal and Mot, god of death and the underworld, begin to rise. Mot does not recognize Baal's reign.

The last section of the Baal Cycle involves a second major conflict (*CAT* 1.5–1.6). This time Baal challenges Mot, the god of death and the underworld. Baal desires to extend his reign over Mot. Thus, they engage in a duel. Baal, however, loses and finds himself trapped in the underworld. His demise leads to parched fields. The gods and goddesses mourn. El and Anat intervene. This leads to the return of Baal from death. Baal and Mot again fight. This time with the help of other deities Baal prevails. But as the annual seasons testify, death and life alternate in their governance of the world. So the Baal cycle ends. Baal is the king who defeated Yamm, but the power of death and the underworld remains a potent threat.

As with all myth, the Baal Epic deals with the deepest fears and longings of humanity. Baal's story focuses primarily on two. First, Baal's conflict with Yamm answers the fear of a catastrophic end of the world as we know it. To elevate Yamm to the pinnacle of power meant the enthronement of chaos and disorder over creation. Yamm personified chaos and served as a constant threat to civilization through the fury of the sea itself as well as through raging rivers and streams whose waters swallowed up travelers and whose floods razed houses and villages. With Baal's defeat of Yamm and the confession, "Baal will reign" comes *security* regarding the future stability of the world. The mighty Storm god Baal would bring life giving rains to the world rather than unleash chaos and destruction. Second, Baal's battle with Mot answers the question of the power of death over life. Mot represented all that opposed life in the world from the loss of vegetation in the winter to the inevitable death of all living beings. In the Baal cycle, these champions fight to a draw. Baal tastes death, but returns alive. Mot then experiences death for a season before emerging anew annually to have his fill. Thus, the Baal Cycle engrains a status quo in which human history records the endless cycles of the seasons of the death and life of all living things.

This worldview comes into direct conflict with the biblical narrative that tells the story of a different God and a new way of understanding reality. Before exploring this, let us ponder the connections between Exodus 15:1b–18 and the Baal Cycle (*CAT* 1.1–1.6).

LINKS BETWEEN THE SONG OF THE SEA AND THE BAAL CYCLE

A close reading of Exodus 15:1b–18 reveals broad narrative parallels with the Baal Cycle as well as close linguistic ties (Craigie 1971:19–26, Cross 1973:112–144, and Russell 2007:39–42 and 69–71). The argument for the connection between Exodus 15:1b–18 and the Baal Cycle does not stand on any one specific piece of data but on the preponderance of evidence.

First, the Song of the Sea narrates the deliverance at the sea, YHWH's guidance of his people to his holy mountain, and final acclamation of YHWH's kingship in roughly the same order as Baal's story:

A. *First Conflict.* Exodus 15:1b–10, 12 narrates YHWH's victory over the forces of Egypt. The sea is not a personification of Yamm, but merely a weapon yielded by YHWH against a human threat to God's people. The Exodus serves as the decisive demonstration of YHWH's power and commitment to God's people throughout Israel's scriptures.

B. *Implied Proclamation of Kingship.* Exodus 15:11 uses the language of incomparability. At this point in the Baal Cycle, Yamm declares Baal king (*CAT* 1.3 III: 28–31). The explicit language of kingship is not present in the Song until 15:18. However the language of incomparability serves a similar function. Mann states that YHWH's elevation over all other gods is nowhere more clear than in Exodus 15:11 (1977:125).

C. *Second Conflict.* Exodus 15:14–16 describes the terror that falls on the peoples of Canaan as YHWH leads his people toward his mountain. These are future enemies. But unlike Mot who proved a worthy and equal opponent to Baal, the peoples of Canaan already stand defeated. They are petrified and as immobile as stones.

D. *Sanctuary on YHWH's Holy Mountain.* Exodus 15:13 and 17 detail YHWH's guidance of God's people to his holy mountain, the mountain of his inheritance. The language of 15:17 mimics the terminology used for Baal's shrine on Zaphan (see below).

E. *Explicit Proclamation of Kingship.* The Song of the Sea reaches its zenith in the confession "YHWH will reign forever and ever." YHWH is king over creation. Unlike the Baal Cycle where a similar confession for Baal occurs in the middle of the story, YHWH stands as unrivaled king at the end of the poem. The declaration of YHWH's eternal rule breaks reality out of the mythic cycles affirmed by Baal's story.

Second, there are two striking linguistic ties that link these two ancient poems.[5] Exodus 15:17 describes YHWH's sacred mountain using the same phraseology as the Baal Cycle deploys in reference to Mount Zaphan (Hess 2007:100, Russell 2007:41, Smith 1997:168n64):

> You brought and planted them *on the mountain of your inheritance,*
> The place for your habitation, you made O YHWH;
> The sanctuary, O YHWH, your hands have established (*italics added,* Exod 15:17)

> Come and I will reveal it, in the midst of my mountain Divine Zaphan
> *In the holy mount of my heritage,*
> In the beautiful hill of my might (*italics added, CAT 1.3 III:28–31*)

Also, the concluding declaration of YHWH's rule (Exod 15:18) is identical to Yamm's words:

> YHWH will reign (Exod 15:18a)
> Baal will reign (*CAT* 1.2 IV:32 and 34–35)

THE SUBVERSION OF BAAL AND THE ELEVATION OF KING YHWH

Once the parallels with the Baal Cycle come to light, readers of the Song of Sea gain insight into the strategy of Israel's great anthem of YHWH's victory at the sea. It functions to instruct God's people in a counter cultural worldview in which they live out their identity as a kingdom of priests and holy nation (Exod 19:5–6) whose vocation is to serve as a conduit of blessing to the nations who do not yet know YHWH (Gen 12:3). Simultaneously, the Song of the Sea proclaims to the nations an alternative vision of reality that serves as an invitation to join God's people in declaring and living in light of YHWH's eternal reign. The Song of the Sea answers the same deep human fears as the Baal Cycle, but its answers articulate a revolutionary worldview central to the rest of scripture and opens up the future to the hope and abundance of God's kingdom. The following features serve as key elements of the Song of the Sea's strategy for undercutting the ideological claims of Baal's story. By deploying language and narrative patterns common to Canaanite religion, the Song of the Sea presents the Gospel of YHWH.

Subversion of the powers behind the gods. In the Song of the Sea, there are only three characters: YHWH, God's people (vv. 13 and 16), and human enemies who threaten God's people (Egypt [esp. vv. 1b and 4], Philistia, Edom, Moab, and the peoples of Canaan [vv. 14–15]). YHWH acts in human history. In the Baal Cycle, events occur in the realm of the gods. It is the story of Baal and Baal's interactions with the pantheon of deities common to the Western Semitic religions. Each of these deities represented a power or force in nature. For example, Yamm was the god of sea and river and Mot was the god of the underworld and death. There is no hint of these gods in Exodus 15. There is only YHWH. In fact, it is striking that YHWH uses two weapons against the Egyptians. In vv. 1b–10, YHWH wields the sea (Heb: *yam*) against Egypt. In YHWH's hands, the sea is not a fearsome deity. It is simply a part of creation that becomes the means by which YHWH defeats Egypt. Likewise v. 12 reports that YHWH opened up the earth and caused it to consume the enemies of God's people. In this context, earth likely takes on the connotation of underworld (Russell 2007: 16). Yet who commands this once feared realm? It is YHWH.

Historicization of Canaanite mythic themes. The good news of the Song of the Sea is the reality that it occurs in human space and time. It is not a tale of the olden days of creation or set in mythic realms. YHWH is active and vibrant in the world on behalf of God's people. YHWH does not fight other gods and goddesses. There is no need. Instead, YHWH fights on behalf of *people* against the superpower of the Late Bronze Age, i.e. Egypt, and neutralizes future enemies in one epic battle at the sea. The Song of the Sea follows the general structure of the Baal Cycle, but narrates the conflicts as a this-world, human-centered account. This is crucial to the rhetorical power of the Song. YHWH does what no other god or goddess does. YHWH acts for *God's people* and does what they could not do for themselves—delivers the weak from the strong. Moreover, the emphasis on God's power over *historical* enemies breaks the mythic cycles. The victory at the Sea was the critical victory necessary to shape a good future for God's people. As noted above, there is not a second enemy to fight in the Song of the Sea. No future battle is needed because God has won all future victories by his demonstration of power at the Sea. Future enemies in Canaan stand frozen in fear before the advance of the people of God.

Pro-Human Vision. In the Baal Cycle, the principal mention of humans occurs in its narration of Anat's murderous rampage against human warriors. The Song of the Sea declares not only that YHWH acts in real human time and space, but that YHWH takes action on behalf of God's people against the human powers of oppression. The God of scripture does not merely move to solidify the *status quo*, which privileges the powerful and sanctifies injustice for the benefit of the few. This was the principal goal and function of ancient myths. They gave ideological support for the power structures as they existed. The official theologies thus blessed and ratified the status quo. The Song of the Sea is radically different. YHWH intercedes, creates, and guides a people who were the opposite of connected and prosperous. In fact, the exaltation of YHWH in the Song of the Sea implies both a new status for and exaltation of God's people (Mann 1977: 129).

Moreover, YHWH desires a *relationship* with this delivered people. They will serve in God's mission, but they are far from slaves in terms of status. In Exodus 15:13 and 17, YHWH brings God's people to the dwelling place of God. This is unprecedented. Baal had a cosmic mountain Zaphan and built a palace there, but he issued no invitations to people. Baal only allowed gods and goddesses to attend his feasts and banquets. YHWH is different. YHWH does not invite deities to the holy mountain. Instead, YHWH invites his newly delivered people. Moderns tend to assume that God, the gods, or the universe works on our behalf for good. We can easily miss the power here. The Song of the Sea not only tells the story of a different kind of god—one who engages our world in order to deliver a people to himself, but it also emphasizes that YHWH the true King (15:18) in fact desires the sort of relationship with God's people that the Near Eastern myths reserved for members of the divine pantheon. Thus, a relational god that cared about common people served as a threat to the power structures of the ancient world. YHWH's victory at the sea and guidance to the sanctuary served as the basis for the identity of God's people. Note the language of the Song of the Sea in vv. 13 and 16: people whom you [YHWH] redeemed (Heb: *ga'al*) and people whom you acquired/created (Heb: *qanah*). The Song does not call the people "Israel." Their identity is in the divine actor who opened up a new future for them.

YHWH's Incomparability. What is the missional message rooted in the unilateral actions of YHWH, the subversion and historicization of mythic themes, and the pro-human agenda? YHWH is incomparable to any other god. In other words, there is no being worthy of the title God and King other than YHWH (Wright, Christopher J. H. 2006:136–142). This is the clear implication of the refrain of v. 11: "Who is like you among the gods, O YHWH? Who is like you mighty among the holy ones? (Miller 1964:241, Muilenberg 1966:244, and Russell 2007:16) Awe-inspiring in praises; doing wonders." As Israel's national anthem, the Song of the Sea lifts up YHWH high above any other divine being.

True Security. The Song of the Sea secures the past, present and future of God's people. Unlike the Baal Cycle, which ends with a cyclical annual sharing of power between Baal and Mot, there is no ambiguity in the witness of the Song about YHWH. YHWH is the king forever—for all seasons and all times. The victory at the Sea and guidance to YHWH's holy mountain ground the security of God's people in the *historical* actions of YHWH on their behalf. God's people are not trapped in endless cycles that codify a suffocating status quo that favors the powerful. The liberating power that saved God's people from Israel and brought them into covenant relationship at Sinai opens up a preferred future in which God's kingdom endures for eternity. Security and deliverance from the deep fears of the dissolution of creation and from the cycles of death and life may be found in YHWH alone. There is no other. In the Baal Cycle, Yamm declares Baal king yet Mot and Baal end the cycle having battled to a stalemate. In contrast, in the Song of the Sea, YHWH's incomparability is evident after the victory at the Sea (15:11). The Song climaxes with the acclamation "YHWH will reign forever and ever." This fully subverts Canaanite myth. There is no cycle of struggle. YHWH's kingship is eternal and not seasonal/cyclical. This is tremendous news for all Creation.

SO WHAT?

The Song of the Sea models a profound understanding of human needs and the communication of transformational truth. Cross and Freedman's description of the song as national anthem captures the power of its language (1955:237n. f). Exodus 15:1b–18 serves as a declaration of YHWH's victory on behalf of God's people following the exodus, but its use of mythic language and themes transcends YHWH's direct intervention in human affairs during the late Bronze age and extends these implications to all who would declare YHWH's eternal kingship. Exodus 15:1b–18 reminds *insiders* of the identity, character, and mission of YHWH. It announces to *outsiders* the incomparability of YHWH and with it an implicit invitation to proclaim with God's people "YHWH will reign."

The ties between the Song of the Sea and the Baal Cycle serve as a missional model for God's twenty-first century people. The deep narratives about the security of the created world as well as the deep fear of death remain part of the human condition. Twenty-first century people may no longer fear gods such as Yamm, but the destructive anti-creational forces personified by Yamm still abide. We moderns fear asteroid strikes, zombie viruses, pandemics, and the threat of catastrophic flooding caused by global warning. We can add to these manmade threats of nuclear devices, electromagnetic pulse weapons, autonomous AI, and totalitarian governments. Of course, the fear of death has never receded from humanity. Moreover, in the twenty-first century, we find the emerging bio-tech field striving to achieve goals of extending human longevity to unprecedented lengths.

These observations demonstrate that the core message of the Song of the Sea remains timely. Wise interpreters of scripture will recognize how the Song's modeling of direct engagement with the late Bronze Age cultural milieu heightened the power of its poetic retelling of YHWH's foundational acts on behalf of God's people. There remains the need to craft compelling retellings of the Gospel in light of the worldviews of the twenty-first century.[6]

END NOTES

[1] Currid does not use the language of missional hermeneutics but still makes a similar argument under the rubric of "polemical theology."

[2] The Baal Cycle includes six tablets (*CAT* 1.1–1.6).

[3] In the Baal Cycle, Yamm carries the twin titles: Prince Sea/Judge River.

[4] This may be the speech of Astarte or perhaps even a final confession by Yamm. The text is fragmentary at this point. Regardless, compare with Exodus 15:18.

[5] Those interested in more data are encouraged to engage the literature referenced at the beginning of this section as there are many more subtle word pairs and shared vocabulary. Given the brevity of this essay, I am only including the two most explicit examples.

[6] I am grateful for the positive influence that Dr. John Oswalt has had on my life. He invested his time and wisdom into me during my years as a student and then as a teaching fellow at Asbury Seminary (1991–96). His modeling of the Christian life and his clear articulation of his scholarly convictions continue to serve as examples for my personal faith and my vocation as an evangelical Wesleyan biblical scholar. It is a privilege to offer this essay in honor of my teacher and mentor.

WORKS CITED

Albright, William F.
1969 *Yahweh and the God's of Canaan*. Garden City: Doubleday.

Craigie, Peter C.
1971 "The Poetry of Ugarit and Israel." *Tyndale Bulletin* 22: 3–31.

Cross, Frank Moore
1973 *Canaanite Myth and Hebrew Epic: Essays in the History and Religion of Israel*. Cambridge, MA: Harvard University Press.

Cross, F. M. and D. N. Freedman
1955 "The Song of Miriam." *JNES* 14: 237–250.

Currid, John D.
2013 *Against the Gods: The Polemical Theology of the Old Testament*. Wheaton, IL: Crossway.

Peter Enns
2005 *Inspiration and Incarnation: Evangelicals and the Problem of the Old Testament*. Grand Rapids: Baker Academic.

Hess, Richard S.
2007 *Israelite Religions: An Archaeological and Biblical Survey*. Grand Rapids: Baker Academic.

Hunsberger, George R.
2016 "Mapping the Missional Hermeneutics Conversation" in *Reading the Bible Missionally* by Michael W. Goheen, ed., 45–67. Grand Rapids: Eerdmans.

Mann, Thomas W.

1977   *Divine Presence and Guidance in Israelite Traditions: The Typology of the Exaltation.* John Hopkins Near Eastern Studies; Baltimore and London: The John Hopkins University Press.

Miller, Patrick D., Jr.

1964   "Two Critical Notes on Psalm 68 and Deuteronomy 33." *HTR* 57: 240–243.

Muilenberg, James

1966   "A Liturgy on the Triumphs of Yahweh" in *Studia Biblical et Semitica: Theodora Christiano Vriezen, 233–251.* Wageningen: Veenman and Zonen.

Oswalt, John

2009   *The Bible among the Myths: Unique Revelation of Just Ancient Literature.* Grand Rapids: Zondervan.

Russell, Brian D.

2016   *(re)Aligning with God: Reading Scripture for Church and World.* Eugene, Or: Cascade Books.

2010   "What is a Missional Hermeneutic." April 1, 2010. Accessed from http://www.catalystresources.org/what-is-a-missional-hermeneutic/.

2007   *The Song of the Sea: The Date of Composition and Influence of Exodus 15:1–21.* Studies in Biblical Literature, 101; New York: Peter Lang.

Smith, Mark

2016   "Ugarit and the Ugaritians" in *The World around the Old Testament: The People and Places of the Ancient Near East* by Bill T. Arnold and Brent A. Strawn, eds, 139–167. Grand Rapids: Baker Academic.

2001   *The Origins of Biblical Monotheism.* Oxford: Oxford University Press.

1997   "The Baal Cycle" in *Ugaritic Narrative Poetry* by Simon B. Parker, ed., 81–180. SBL Writings from the Ancient World, 9; Atlanta: Scholars Press.

Wright, Christopher J. H.
2006   *The Mission of God: Unlocking the Bible's Grand Narrative.* Downer's Grove: InterVarsity Press.

Wright, G. Ernest
1950   *The Old Testament Against Its Environment.* London: SCM Press.

"I'm Gonna Make You Famous": Joshua 6:23-27

LAWSON G. STONE

KEYWORDS:

fame, Ramses II, Joshua, Bronze Age, monuments

Lawson G. Stone (PhD, Yale University) is Professor of Old Testament at Asbury Theological Seminary in Wilmore, Kentucky.

Abstract

"So the LORD was with Joshua, and his fame was in all the land.
(Josh 6:27)

The greatest of the Egyptian Pharaohs, Ramses II provides a dramatic foil highlighting the Old Testament presentation of the figure of Joshua, a contemporary of Ramses. The accomplishments of each gave them reason to believe their contributions would be lasting, but ultimately only one changed the world, while the other was largely forgotten except by historians and archaeologists. The fame of Ramses arose from his arrogant exercise of power, while the fame of Joshua was bestowed on him as a faithful successor of Moses in serving YHWH.

One of the most conspicuous features of the legacy of John N. Oswalt is his biblical preaching. His ability to focus the vital life of the biblical story and juxtapose it with contemporary experience consistently challenges and delights those who hear him. This is a sermon preached at Asbury Theological Seminary October 18, 2016. I wrote this sermon thinking of my professor and mentor, who also introduced me to Shelly's poem "Ozymandias" which he would recite from memory in class.

Introduction

Fame. It's probably one of the two or three most sought-after prizes in our world. Whether it's a horde of "friends" on Facebook, a posse of followers on Twitter, or maybe it's bigger – book sales, high profile speaking engagements, prominence in denominational leadership… Fame makes the other things people seek after just that much better. Nobody much likes to admit that they want fame, but deep down, most of us do.

Fame was important in the ancient world. Monuments, inscriptions, temples, massive burial complexes, palaces, capital cities were built on bedrock just across the river from the existing, perfectly functional capital. Fame drove the kings, warlords and elites of the ancient world every bit as much as it drives us today, and even more so, because they believed that fame in this world also made you famous with the gods! They feared that if their name was forgotten, somehow in the afterlife they would suffer or experience annihilation.

Every ancient monarch tried to put up as many monuments and inscriptions as they could, all inscribed with their name, and at the end, a declaration that anyone who defaces their name, replaces it on the monument, or just allows it to fall into disrepair and not be visible, will be punished by terrible curses! Likewise, those who ensure the monument's visibility, keep it prominent, will be blessed and at times could add a supplementary inscription with his own name, or just add his name to the restored inscription.[1]

So when YHWH says to Joshua, "I'm going to make you famous!" he was saying a lot more than "you're going to be trending on Twitter for a month!" Spoken to any aspiring leader in the ancient world, God was promising success in every endeavor, everlasting remembrance, eternal recognition of his exploits. A name above all names, a name at which every knee would bow… Or was it?

Ramses II: Poster Boy for Ancient Fame

Travel back in time with me in your imagination. The scene I'm sketching is based on facts, but with some elaboration as well. The year is 1258 BC.[2] The place is Per-Ramses, Egypt. A 40-something Egyptian pharaoh looks across his capital city. It is a splendid, sprawling capital. Built on the older site of the Hyksos capital of Avaris, refurbished by his grandfather, further developed by his father, the construction efforts of Ramses II ensured that this city is thought to be one of the largest, if not the largest single, integrally constructed building on the face of the earth prior to the modern era. Excavations by the archaeologist Manfred Bietak at the site known as Qantir, or Tel-ed-Dab'a, confirm this. The city proper was over 3.7 miles long and 2 miles wide, and enclosed well over 2500 acres,[3] That's 10 million square meters! It was criss-crossed by canals and lakes, and has been called the "Venice of Ancient Egypt." The site was so stupendous, it's even mentioned in the Bible as the great city on which the Israelite slaves had labored.

In the distance Ramses spots 3 splendidly arrayed chariots, clearly a diplomatic dispatch, accompanied by a retinue of retainers, recorders, sycophants and camp followers. The Pharaoh, Ramses II, smiles, and for good reason. He is ending a 250-year war with the only remaining super-power of the ancient world. He is about to make an everlasting peace with the Hittite king Hatush-Ili III. Months of delicate negotiations have brought about this momentous achievement: the two most dangerous military and imperial powers of the Late Bronze Age are about to make peace!

But Ramses II knows that more than negotiations led to this moment. His mind travels back some 15 or 16 years, back to the city of Kadesh on the Orontes, in the year 1274 BC. Then a 20-something new king of Egypt, Ramses II, looks down on a field of battle. Caught by surprise during a rash, unguarded and hasty advance when he'd divided his force and been duped by Hittite spies, he'd been attacked by surprise after making camp. He'd been trapped between the walls of Kadesh and the waters of the Orontes River. He and his army faced almost certain annihilation.

But...the young king showed his mettle and through fierce personal, raw physical courage, enormous skill handling his chariot, and lethal effectiveness with his personal weaponry, fought back, rallied his troops, and staved off utter disaster.[4]

Ramses didn't win. But he didn't have to. All he had to do was fight to a draw. Which is what he did.

Before him is the carnage of the battlefield. Wrecked chariots, dead horses, dead men, now stripped of their armor and weapons, being loaded for whatever burial they would get.

But something monumental had happened. All through the Late Bronze Age, the great powers had fenced and feinted at one another, masking their hostility behind diplomatic exchanges and predatory trade-deals, always fighting each other via proxies, their client kings in Canaan and Syria.

But this day, almost by mistake, the two great kings, Ramses II of Egypt and Muwatalli II of the Hittites, met *directly* on the field of battle, their *full* forces engaged. It was as if the United States and Russia collided on the battlefield of Syria, fully deployed, fully committed, locked and loaded, safeties off, nuclear codes keyed in. And disaster was averted, albeit after a brutal, bloody battle.

The young Ramses had negotiated a cease-fire with the Hittite king. Both men had decided to go home and tell a tale of victory so glorious only the gods could have given it; or god-kings. Both men decided to let the other one get away with it.

Both men clearly knew they had in the other not just a formidable adversary, but also, someone with whom they could deal. Terms were reached.

It had taken 16 more years, a Hittite leadership crisis, the rise of a new empire in the east and a new Hittite king, but today, the Hittite chariots were bearing solid silver tablets inscribed, in elegant Mesopotamian cuneiform, the first known written peace treaty between two world-class super-powers, including an agreement, by the way, to return any fugitive escaped slaves that might stumble onto their territory.

So watching those chariots approaching, in his 40's, Ramses believed that he'd secured a peace that would last forever. He felt he had reached the pinnacle of influence, power, beneficence, and fame and that the whole world had opened up before him, a future of Egyptian-fostered peace; wealth, power and fame seemed inevitable. Among the many temples, inscriptions, monuments and statues that Ramses II raised for himself, to promote his fame and everlasting memory, one was over 30 feet high, carved from a single stone, and weighed over 80 tons.

What Ramses did not know was that the world for which he had secured peace was about to vanish. The Bronze Age culture, which had stood for thousands of years, achieved a pinnacle of splendor, wealth, sophistication and power in his own person and rule. But now it was about to explode into a million shards and fly across the land, then be blown away in the wind and covered with dust.[5]

The end of the Late Bronze Age was so traumatic, so cataclysmic, that historians refer to it as "The Catastrophe." Ramses died after an epic, 67-year rule, in 1212 BC. A dozen years later, it was all over. A darkness of confusion, violence, destruction, and chaos descended on the ancient Near East, with no relief coming for 200 years. Egypt didn't fall. It just shriveled. From the Sun God of the ancient world, Egypt dwindled to a flickering lamp in a hurricane. Within a generation, the Egyptians would abandon the land of Canaan and hunker down in their traditional homeland; a mere shadow of the power they had been, never, ever again to emerge as a world-class power. By the time of Samuel and Saul, Ramses' great capital city had been abandoned. The branch of the Nile River upon which it had been built silted up, and the Venice of Egypt found itself with no water, an instant ghost town. The capital shifted, stones and monuments were robbed out of the abandoned ruins, and the sands, the eternally victorious desert sands, covered the site. The name "Ramses" would continue to be borne by the great king's descendants, but none would equal his stature, and the glorious city he built was all but forgotten.[6]

Ramses thought he'd done something great, but it was over in a blink of the eye.

That's the fame of the world.

Joshua: A Different Type of Fame?

Now, let's leave Ramses in peace back at his capital, contemplating a new world order, everlasting fame, and 1000-ton collosi, and think ahead a few years, about 1240 BC.[7]

Another man, Joshua, faces a challenge. This man is no Ramses, though he's about the same age. But he's from the entirely other end of the social spectrum. This man is not a mighty king. He has no capital city, no golden chariots, no retainers. Instead of solid silver tablets inscribed with dozens of lines of ornate cuneiform, he has two rough tables of stone inscribed with a few lines of primitive Hebrew script, some scrolls, and his memory of a great man: Moses. Joshua is a former slave of Egypt. In Egypt's eyes, in the eyes of the great Ramses, he is a fugitive from justice. He has to guide his people, all escaped slaves and the children of slaves, across the torrential flood of the Jordan river, and take on the city-rulers of Canaan—about 30 of these kings, all in the employ of... Ramses... all devoted to advancing the power of Egypt and their own careers. They will not stand by and allow the Israelites to return to the land where their ancestors, Abraham, Isaac, and Jacob, had lived, which was promised to them by YHWH. Not a chance. Though Canaan is, in the grand scheme of things, a backwater, and these town rulers were pretty much third-rate warlords, to a rag-tag army of former slaves coming in from the desert, these town rulers pose a lethal threat. They are better armed, better trained, better supplied. They are professional soldiers, many foreign mercenaries. Every one would have been committed to destroying these escaped slaves or returning them, like the fugitives they were, to Egypt.[8] In the service of Egypt's voracious appetites, these rulers had systematically stripped the land of its agricultural produce, steadily reduced the peasant population to desperation, subjected them to forced labor, and expatriated thousands to Egypt to serve the Pharaoh.[9] They are accustomed to stomping the daylights out of peasant uprisings and third-rate revolutionaries. To them, Israel, poorly armed, ill-trained, is at this moment, a mere annoyance. Israel is out-gunned before they even enter the land.

To this man, Joshua, God offers *to make him famous!*

Is the fame that God will offer Joshua really the same thing as that sought by all the great ones of the ancient—and face it, modern—world?

The book of Joshua shows how God went about making Joshua famous.

First of all, Joshua actually needed something of a public relations branding boost: look who he had to follow, Moses! The Babylonian Talmud observes, "The elders of that generation said: The countenance of Moses was like that of the sun; the countenance of Joshua was like that of the moon. Alas, for such shame! Alas for such reproach!"[10] Moses, who faced down Pharaoh, presided over the divinely-sent barrage of plagues, led the nation out of slavery, crossed the Red Sea, stood before God at Sinai, received the Ten Commandments (twice!), and mediated the covenant between YHWH and his people. This Moses is called "The Servant of YHWH," which is the highest accolade an Old Testament character can receive! And yet, Joshua, in the first verse of his book, is called "the assistant of Moses" and even though Moses is dead, he, not Joshua, is still called "The Servant of YHWH." So Joshua needs some elevation. Israel was in a stature crisis. As the memory of Moses faded—which it did if the book of Judges is any indication—who would be the next person to wear those sandals?

Joshua also needed a publicity boost because the text hints that for some in Israel, Joshua was somewhat on trial. When he challenges the tribes settling east of the Jordan River to cross over and fight with their fellow Israelites west of Jordan, they answer, "Sure, we'll do it, we'll obey you just like we obeyed Moses, as long as the Lord is with you the same way he was with Moses!" I've adjusted the translation there a tad so you can hear the emphasis in the original. It's not well wishes! It's a condition, indeed, a *sine qua non*, almost an ultimatum: we'll follow you like we followed Moses, BUT, you had better be someone whom the Lord is with, the same way he was with Moses.

That's why it's vital to notice that God really does give Joshua prestige and favor in the eyes of the people. As they cross the Jordan it its full flood stage, a huge and dangerous undertaking, the narrator tells us, "Now the LORD said to Joshua, "This day I will begin to exalt you in the sight of all Israel, that they may know that just as I have been with Moses, I will be with you" (Josh. 3:7). Then as they complete the passage of the Jordan, we are told, "On that day the LORD exalted Joshua in the sight of all Israel; so that they revered him, just as they had revered Moses all the days of his life" (Josh. 4:14). And then after the victory at Jericho, we read the words I chose as an epigraph over this reflection: "So the LORD was with Joshua, and his fame was in all the land."

But for Joshua, fame is not really the goal. Fame was just a means to a larger purpose. After they cross the Jordan, Joshua reminds the people that their actions are so that "all the peoples of the earth may know the hand of the LORD, that it is mighty, so that you may fear the LORD your God forever" (Josh 4:24). Later people will speak not of hearing of Joshua's fame, but of hearing the mighty deeds of YHWH.

So how does that work out for Joshua?

Run ahead 5 years. This man, Joshua, stands on a hilltop. This time, it's in the north of Canaan, on the heights of Naphtali. From these heights, about 2500 feet above sea level he can look down about 1400 feet to the great citadel of Hazor. This town is the crown jewel of Canaan. The Bible calls it "The head of all those kingdoms." It's ruler alone, among all the rulers of Canaan's towns and cities, got away with calling himself, in letters to the great rulers, a "king" (rather than "mayor"). As Hazor goes, so goes the entire northern third of Canaan, all of the Galilee. Joshua has led his people's fighting force, all former slaves of Egypt, in a series of pitched battles against the Thug rulers and Warlords of Canaan.

The escaped slave, Joshua and his fighting force of escaped slaves, knew they could never have their old home of Canaan back, knew that nobody could ever live in peace in Canaan, as long as these Thugs, these petty gangster-kings of Canaan, had their way.

The Bible says, "His fame was in all the land." But seriously, for Canaan, that's not saying much. It's like saying "He was famous all over Lake Wobegon!" Here at the end, just as in the beginning, Joshua has to remember that the battle, as, ultimately, does the fame, belongs to the Lord.

So he'd waged a series of battles aimed at decapitating Ramses' administration in Canaan. The rulers of Jericho, Ai, Lachish, Ashkelon, Azekah, and many others—30 in all—had joined together to stop him. All failed.

And now, looking down on the daunting 200 acre city of Hazor, Joshua can tell his compatriots: this is the last one. When this city falls, the campaign is over. Canaan will be free from Egypt's tyranny. It will be able to breathe again. The blood of centuries of civil war and imperial oppression will wash from its soil. The fields trampled every year by horses, chariots, wagons and carts, the boots of thousands of soldiers, will blossom with crops and flowers. Roads once choked by military convoys will bustle with commerce.

The Israelites would do something they had fantasized about for generations: They would *farm*, on their own land. They would hand that farm to their children, secure in the knowledge that their great king, YHWH, unlike Ramses, happily gave them the land and would ensure they could keep it. They would live kindly on the land, not stripping it, not wrenching from it every single morsel it could produce, leaving it tired and depleted. They would live kindly on it. And the land would reward their kindness with bounty.

Canaan's highland fields only yielded crops to those with discerning minds and sensitive hands, who could be intimate with the land and fit the cultivation technique precisely to each little patch of soil. Now this land would begin to support hundreds of small farming villages and towns popping up after about 1200 BC, like mushrooms after a spring rain.

These former slaves, these peasants born in the wilderness of Sinai, Edom, and Moab, would do something daring: they would *plant vineyards*, which needed years to mature. They would plant olive trees, which couldn't yield for a generation. Such plantings say they could imagine a future, a future without Ramses or his Thug-Princes.

And this Joshua, looking down at Hazor, probably knew the great powers of his age, the Late Bronze Age, were doomed. He knew the restiveness of groups on the move, the Philistines, the Moabites, the Ammonites, the little kingdoms, the mice in a game of big cats; but mice growing claws and teeth. But he didn't need pundits and researchers, he knew this because he knew his God. YHWH, the Lord of Hosts, the God of Israel, had declared his promise, a promise that gave Israel hope. And YHWH's law, especially as seen in Deuteronomy, had cast a vision for a completely new society, one in which Kings were not tyrants, but guardians of the covenant, the alliance binding YHWH with his people, and binding his people one with another. A society in which each person considered the other a brother or a sister, where each family would be a sacred enclosure, safe from predation and violation. Where each person's land would be inviolate. Where one day each week was devoted to rest and celebration. Where life, truth, honor, marriage and family were the highest goods. Where God alone was truly king, and the human king was simply his glad and humble steward, as was prophesied by Jacob in Genesis: "The scepter will not depart from Judah, *until he comes to whom it belongs*" (Gen 49:10). The king in Israel was merely a steward, a humble custodian of the authority that ultimately belonged to God.

This Joshua! Really, he was a nobody. He came from nobody we know. I like to joke that Joshua the son of Nun was the "Son of None" because we have no idea who "Nun" was. Joshua left behind no descendants we can identify. The text reports no marriage, no children, though according to the Talmud, Joshua married… Rahab the Harlot![11] I like to hope that's true! But we don't really know. Once the little patch of ground promised to Israel was secured, Joshua retired from soldiering. No life in campaign tents for him. No triumphant marches trailing spoils and captives from foreign wars would commemorate Joshua. By every single measure of ancient Near Eastern grandeur – land, cities, ancestry, offspring, palatial residences, worldwide conquest and domination, monumental inscriptions – Joshua was ultimately a loser. No kingdom, no glory, no wealth, no palaces, no descendants.

Then, this Joshua did something Ramses would never have done, that no self-respecting world-class ruler would do. *He just vanished.* He retired to his own patch of ground, inherited by divine lot, like everyone else. He farmed, for how long exactly, we don't know. We do know he emerged again at the age of 110 years to give a speech, and then to die.

A nobody.

No Ramses II is he.

And yet, this old earth would circle the sun over 3200 more times, and the name of Joshua would still be known and celebrated. But really, other than historians, who knows of Ramses II? He has become a cinema cartoon character, Yule Brenner in eye-liner, moaning "Moses, Moses, Moses!" Who recalls the name of the Hittite king he made his peace with? And what happened to that everlasting treaty of peace?

In 1818 the British Museum announced that it would be receiving a 7.25-ton fragment of a massive statue of Ramses II. It would be 3 more years before this treasure arrived, but the announcement, and the fact that this massive statue had been hidden in the desert sands for thousands of years, inspired the poet, Percy Shelly, to pen one of his most famous poems, using one of Ramses' throne names, in an anglicized form, "Ozymandias:"

> I met a traveller from an antique land
> Who said: "Two vast and trunkless legs of stone
> Stand in the desert. Near them, on the sand,
> Half sunk, a shattered visage lies, whose frown,
> And wrinkled lip, and sneer of cold command,
> Tell that its sculptor well those passions read
> Which yet survive, stamped on these lifeless things,
> The hand that mocked them and the heart that fed:
> And on the pedestal these words appear:
> 'My name is Ozymandias, king of kings:
> Look on my works, ye Mighty, and despair!'
> Nothing beside remains. Round the decay
> Of that colossal wreck, boundless and bare
> The lone and level sands stretch far away.

Statue of Ramses II in the British Museum

(image used with permission)

Joshua, the nobody, son of nobody, is immortalized in scripture. More importantly, when God decided to become an actual human being, to enter into this tired, dying world and breathe new life into it, when God took on flesh to suffer and die and rise again for the redemption of creation, when he decided, like

Joshua, to lead a host of captives into a far greater promised land, to save his people from their sins, he took a name:

"And they shall call his name, Jesus." In Hebrew, Joshua.

Which prompts me to ask: *who are we trying to be?* Ramses, or Joshua? In whose eyes do we seek to be famous? In the eyes of the world and its gangster-princes and thug-princesses? Do we seek the fame of power, wealth, politics, big churches with giant budgets and sprawling campuses... awards, accolades, media attention, thousands of people hanging on our every word? Do we imagine that a thousand years from now, our legacy will live on if we just get a little more wealth, a little more power, a little ...whatever?

Somewhere, a breeze is already blowing, ready to cover our monuments with sand. In the world's fame, the sand always wins.

Joshua's fame was known throughout the land, and for all eternity.

Ramses is known to historians as the greatest of all the kings who had no clue how soon it would all be over.

In whose eyes do we seek fame? Which audience is the one for which we play?

END NOTES

[1] Cf. S. Richter, *The Deuteronomistic History and the Name Theology: lĕšakkēn šĕmô šām in the Bible and the Ancient Near East* (BZAW 318; Berlin: Walter de Gruyter, 2002), 134-135. 179-182. For the less common practice of a king writing his own name alongside a predecessor while restoring monuments, cf. the inscription of Ashur-Resh-Ishi I. (Grayson, A. K. *Assyrian Rulers of the Third and Second Millenia BC [to 1115 BC]* [Toronto: University of Toronto, 1987] 314.

[2] For the life of Ramses II, see K. A. Kitchen, *Pharaoh Triumphant: The Life and Times of Ramessess II* (Warminster: Aris & Phillips, 1982); and more briefly, idem, "Pharaoh Ramesses II and his Times," in *Civilizations of the Ancient Near East*, ed. J. Sasson (Peabody: Hendrickson, 2006; orig. Scribners pub. 1995), 2:763-774.

[3] Marc Van De Mierup, *The Eastern Mediterranean in the Age of Ramses II* (Oxford: Blackwell, 2007) 73-74.

[4] For Ramses' account: W. W. Hallo, ed. *The Context of Scripture.* 3 vols. Leiden: Brill, 2003) II:32-40 and the *editio princeps*: A. Gardiner, *The Kadesh Inscriptions of Ramesses II* (Oxford: Griffith Institute, 1960).

[5] For summary with extensive bibliography, cf. L. G. Stone, "Early Israel and Its Appearance in Canaan," in *Ancient Israel's History: An Introduction to Issues and Sources*, ed. B. T. Arnold and R. S. Hess (Grand Rapids: Baker, 2014), 138-142. Most significant studies include: William A. Ward and Martha Sharp Joukowsky, eds., *The Crisis Years: The 12th Century From Beyond the Danube to the Tigris* (Dubuque, IA: Kendall/Hunt Publishing, 1989); Robert Drews, *The End of the Bronze Age: Changes in Warfare and the Catastrophe of ca 1200 BC*, (Princeton, 1993); E. Cline, *1177 BC: The Year Civilization Collapsed.* (Princeton: Princeton University, 2014).

[6] J. Weinstein, "The Collapse of the Egyptian Empire in the Southern Levant," in Ward and Joukowsky, *The Crisis Years*, 142-150; I. Singer, "Egyptians, Canaanites, and Philistines in the Period of the Emergence of Israel," in Israel Finkelstein and

Nadav Na'aman, eds. *From Nomadism to Monarchy: Archaeological and Historical Aspects of Early Israel* (Jerusalem: Israel Exploration Society, 1994) 282-338; L. H. Lesko, "Egypt in the 12th Century," in Ward and Joukowsky, *The Crisis Years*, 151-156.

[7] For the chronology of Israelite origins, cf. L. G. Stone, "Early Israel and Its Appearance," 130-38.

[8] Repatriation of escaped slaves was a standard provision in treaty texts, such that T. Bryce, (*Letters of the Great Kings of the Ancient Near East: The Royal Correspondence of the Late Bronze Age* [London: Routledge, 2003], 86-93, 213-217) concludes Hittite failed usurper Urhi Teshub must have fled to Egypt prior to the treaty of 1258 B.C., though the Hittite king still threatened Ramses with "another Qadesh."

[9] J. Weinstein, "The Egyptian Empire in Palestine: A Reassessment," *BASOR* 241 (1981): 1-28; N. Na'aman, "Economic Aspects of the Egyptian Occupation of Canaan," *Canaan in the Second Millenium B.C.E. Collected Essays, Volume 2* (Winona Lake: Eisenbrauns, 2005), 216-231, orig. pub. 1981; N. Na'aman, "Pharaonic Lands in the Jezreel Valley in the Late Bronze Age," *Canaan in the Second Millenium*, 232-241, orig. pub. 1988.

[10] Baba Bathra, 75b.

[11] Talmud, b. Meg. 14b. Naturally this tradition triggered multi-generational debate in rabbinic commentary about the legitimacy of Joshua's marriage to a woman of Canaan.

Works Cited

Bryce, T.
    2003   *Letters of the Great Kings of the Ancient Near East: The Royal Correspondence of the Late Bronze Age*. London: Routledge.

Cline, E.
    2014   *1177 BC: The Year Civilization Collapsed*. Princeton: Princeton University.

Drews, Robert
    1993   *The End of the Bronze Age: Changes in Warfare and the Catastrophe of ca 1200 BC*. Princeton, Princeton University.

Gardiner, A. ed.
    1960   *The Kadesh Inscriptions of Ramesses II*. Oxford: Griffith Institute.

Grayson, A. K.
    1987   *Assyrian Rulers of the Third and Second Millenia BC [to 1115 BC]*. Toronto: University of Toronto.

Hallo, W.W., ed.
    2003   *The Context of Scripture*. 3 vols. Leiden: Brill.

Kitchen, K.A.
    2006(1995) "Pharaoh Ramesses II and his Times," in *Civilizations of the Ancient Near East*, ed. J. Sasson (Peabody: Hendrickson, 2006; orig. Scribners pub. 1995, 2:763-774).

    1982   *Pharaoh Triumphant: The Life and Times of Ramessess II*. Warminster: Aris & Phillips.

Lesko, L.H.

1989 "Egypt in the 12th Century," in Ward and Joukowsky, *The Crisis Years: The 12th Century From Beyond the Danube to the Tigris.* Dubuque, IA: Kendall/Hunt Publishing, pp.151-156.

Na'aman, N.

2005a "Economic Aspects of the Egyptian Occupation of Canaan," in *Canaan in the Second Millenium B.C.E. Collected Essays, Volume 2.* Winona Lake: Eisenbrauns, pp. 216-231.

2005b "Pharaonic Lands in the Jezreel Valley in the Late Bronze Age," if *Canaan in the Second Millenium Collected Essays, Volume 2.* Winona Lake: Eisenbrauns, pp. 232-241.

Richter, S.

2002 *The Deuteronomistic History and the Name Theology: lĕšakkēn šĕmô šām in the Bible and the Ancient Near East* (BZAW 318; Berlin: Walter de Gruyter).

Stone, L.G.

2014 "Early Israel and Its Appearance in Canaan," in *Ancient Israel's History: An Introduction to Issues and Sources*, ed. B. T. Arnold and R. S. Hess (Grand Rapids: Baker, 2014), pp. 130-142.

Singer, I.

1994 "Egyptians, Canaanites, and Philistines in the Period of the Emergence of Israel," in Israel Finkelstein and Nadav Na'aman, eds. *From Nomadism to Monarchy: Archaeological and Historical Aspects of Early Israel.* Jerusalem: Israel Exploration Society, pp. 282-338.

Van De Mierup, Marc

2007 *The Eastern Mediterranean in the Age of Ramses II.* Oxford: Blackwell.

Weinstein, J.
  1981   "The Egyptian Empire in Palestine: A Reassessment,"
          BASOR 241: 1-28.

  1989   "The Collapse of the Egyptian Empire in the Southern
          Levant," in Ward and Joukowsky, *The Crisis Years: The 12th
          Century From Beyond the Danube to the Tigris*. Dubuque, IA:
          Kendall/Hunt Publishing, pp. 142-150.

Ward, William A. and Martha Sharp Joukowsky, eds.
  1989   *The Crisis Years: The 12th Century From Beyond the Danube to
          the Tigris*. Dubuque, IA: Kendall/Hunt Publishing.

Yet Another Try on Job 42:6[1]

DAVID L. THOMPSON

KEYWORDS:

Job, dust and ashes, repentance, human nature

David L. Thompson (PhD, Johns Hopkins University) is Professor Emeritus of Biblical Studies at Asbury Theological Seminary in Wilmore, Kentucky.

Abstract

This paper examines the find statement of Job in response to YHWH's speech, which is often translated as "Therefore I despise myself, and repent in dust and ashes." This paper argues that there are problems with the translation, with the Hebrew for "relent" being used, and not the word for "repent." It also argues from other uses of the expression "dust and ashes" that this may be a phrase used to refer to Job's humanity. In this sense, Job agrees that he has spoken beyond his competence with YHWH and relents regarding in the weakness of his humanity, which is not a sin, or something for which repentance is necessary.

INTRODUCTION

In most English versions Job 42:6 reads: "Therefore I despise myself, and repent in dust and ashes." These are Job's last words in the book of Job, the final lines of his response to YHWH's second speech (42:1-6). These are the words for which the readers have been waiting for forty chapters. They contain the conclusion Job draws ("therefore"/ עַל־כֵּן) to everything that has preceded it in this magisterial work, and they appear to present a thoroughgoing repudiation of himself and presumably also his claims throughout the book. He assumes his speeches have morally offended the Almighty. For this and no doubt more he repents, groveling in the ashes he has inhabited since YHWH's attack on his body in chapter². In spite of God's barrage of questions, he has not really answered Job and does not plan to. Some such interpretation commonly flows from this reading of the verse.

Three or four major interpretive decisions have to be made to get to this or any other rendering of the text.

- First, one has to discern the meaning of מאס in 6a. What does the writer claim Job is or does? If he commits an action, to whom does he do it?

- Second, what does נחמתי mean here? "I Repent? "I Relent," or something else?

- Third, what about the prepositional phrase? How does על qualify נחמתי? And what does "dust and ashes"/ עפר ואפר mean?

PROBLEMS WITH THE TRADITIONAL TRANSLATION

The construal expressed in this translation ("I repent in dust and ashes.") has had wide currency. Among English versions the ESV, RSV, NRSV, KJV, NKJV, NIV all have "I despise myself" or the like, as does the Vulgate and the LXX (with additional material). Translating "I repent..." are the Vulgate, KJV, NKJV, NASB, ESV, NAB, RSV, NRSV, NIV, and REB (cf. NLT). The same versions understand the prepositional phrase as indicating the place where or perhaps the mode in which Job repents—"in dust and ashes." This same rendering appears in a recent *Biblia Santa*. The new Korean Revised Version, goes a slightly different path in 6a, but translates 6b, "I repent in dust and ashes."

But "I repent in dust and ashes" is an unfortunate translation of נחמתי על־עפר ואפר. How this reading has been preserved as the majority reading in the English tradition I do not really understand. Two critical difficulties with this translation strike one immediately. First, so far as I can tell, נחמתי על cannot mean, "I repent in X." The Niphal of נחם does not mean "repent" in the sense of "turning away from a breach of moral law," "turning away from sin." That would be שוב. Rather, in the Niphal, נחם means "to change one's mind." Sometimes this carries with it a degree of regret for the action one relents from doing (as in Gen 6:6.). But just as often, as in Jonah 3:10, נחם carries no overtone of regret. Here, "having seen how the Ninevites "turned" (שוב) from their wicked ways, YHWH "relented" (נחם). That is, he changed his mind regarding the judgment he had planned to do and did not do it. In this case it appears YHWH was happy to change his mind, happy to turn from judgment to mercy, which he had desired all along to show to Nineveh. The term נחם here involved no regret.

But what does "relent regarding dust and ashes" mean? (This puzzle may be the reason the traditional translation, which seems to be obvious and clear, has persisted.) We deal here with a set expression, not a string of discrete terms. By themselves each of the terms is clear enough. The term עָפָר means "dust" or "dirt" of the ground, and אֵפֶר means "the residue from burning something." Together "dust and ashes"— עָפָר וָאֵפֶר – in that order, *could* refer to the stuff they would designate separately. Thus Ben Sira 40:3 has a man humbled "in dust and ashes." Sadly, we do not have a Hebrew *vorlage* for this line in Ben Sira, so we do not know whether it carried a preposition or not, and if it did, what it was.

Finding Traction on a Solution

In the OT the phrase עָפָר וָאֵפֶר occurs three times: once in Genesis (18:27), twice in Job. The Genesis occurrence is informative. Here YHWH and Abraham stand face to face in conversation (negotiation?) regarding the justice of God's destroying the righteous along with the wicked of Sodom. Abraham shows proper deference to YHWH, recognizing him as Judge of All the Earth whom one can surely assume will do right. Still, at each stage of the conversation it is Abraham who has taken the initiative and the higher moral ground in suggesting a course of action to YHWH. He says he has taken it upon himself to speak as he has, *even though* he is "dust and ashes"/ עָפָר וָאֵפֶר. Here Abraham acknowledges his own profound distance from YHWH in terms of status and credentials for giving moral guidance to the Judge of All the Earth. He lives in fewer and less cosmic dimensions than does the Judge of All the Earth. He acknowledges his humanity in all its finitude and limitations. Even so, Abraham has YHWH's respect as one to whom he has made far reaching promises and with whom he shares accountability for the actualization of those promises (Gen 18:19, 25, 27). We recall the famous *Tiqune Soferim* (one of eighteen prescribed scribal corrections) had YHWH *standing before Abraham* in 18:22. Abraham's constitution and status as עָפָר וָאֵפֶר here is clearly nothing for which to express regret or guilt. It may actually provide part of the resources that allow Abraham to speak as he has. Even though he observes proper ettiquette in his speaking to a superior, he nevertheless proceeds to speak with confidence that he will survive the encounter.

In Job 30:19, Job says "God has cast me in the mire, and I have become like עָפָר וָאֵפֶר." Job has become like one whose human frailty and finitude are painfully obvious to all who see him. Here עָפָר וָאֵפֶר names a state of dishonor and community disdain. There was a time, however, when it was not so. There was a time when he apparently was not so obviously עָפָר וָאֵפֶר. But the radical change from Job chapter 29 to Job 30 is laid out. There was a time when Job lived like a king among his troops, one who comforted others (29:25). But now, the text emphasizes the change, he is mocked by people his junior, men whose fathers would not even have run with Job's sheepdogs (30:1). One assessment of this new, inferior social status is that "[God] has thrown [him] into the mud. [He is] nothing more than dust and ashes." Our text, Job 42:6, has the only other occurrence of עָפָר וָאֵפֶר. It may help us to consider briefly other aspects of YHWH's speeches that bear on our verse.

First, the writer introduces these speeches as "responses" to Job, using the same rubric as seen before to introduce the speeches of Job and his friends. Ordinarily these "answers" contained a brief, opening direct answer to the preceding speaker and then more extended presentation of less directly related themes. The writer apparently thinks these speeches of YHWH do respond to Job in some way, no matter how modern critics may complain. Job has repeatedly asked that he might argue his case directly to God, and that God would respond to him face to face, bringing a clear indictment and explaining exactly what Job has done that has produced the assault God has leveled at Job.

To this request/challenge YHWH responds with two primary accusations. According to YHWH, Job has spoken beyond his competence, bringing more confusion than clarity to the dialogues (38:2). In addition, and more seriously, Job has maligned God in an attempt to justify his own behavior (40:2, 8). Job agrees with YHWH's charge that Job has spoken beyond his competence: "I'm nothing—how could I ever find the answers," (40:4 NLT) and "I was talking about things about which I knew nothing" (42:3, NLT). Beyond these two items YHWH ignores the specific content of Job's speeches. This leaves open the charge that he has slandered God in the process of justifying himself.

YHWH's directions to Job are enlightening. Before both speeches YHWH says he is going to interrogate Job, and he challenges Job to enlighten him (38:3; 40:7). He says Job should prepare for this interrogation by "girding up [his] loins like a real man (a *geber*)." HALOT, 28, takes this expression, "Gird up the loins," to mean preparation for battle, including preparation for metaphorical battle; i.e., a debate. In Jer 1:17, in a situation similar to our Job setting, YHWH tells Jeremiah to "gird up [his] loins" in order to speak boldly in the face of the recalcitrant and hostile audience in Judah. He is to rise to the challenge of his vocation. He is not to be overcome by his fear.

In Job 38:3 and 40:7 YHWH tells Job to gird up loins in preparation for a situation where YHWH will interrogate and Job will need to inform the Almighty. Job has called repeatedly for just such a hearing (finally and directly in 31:35-37; cf 27:11). YHWH here responds to his demand. This is now a legal contest in which the two are engaged, in which Job will need to speak to a legal adversary and respond well. YHWH urges Job to respond as a *geber* to the direct and indirect accusations of YHWH and to the claims implicit in the questions. He does not have to respond as one of the creatures who entered the heavenly court to stand before YHWH in chapter 1 (1:6-12). Nor need he answer as the Satan or as one of the בני־האלהים. Instead he is to answer as a *geber*, the vigorous man that he is.

It is not expected that he will explain matters obviously beyond his control or beyond his competence as a *geber*. It is a foregone conclusion that he will not be able to answer any of the questions he is asked. YHWH does direct him, however, to respond adequately as a *geber*. This he apparently does, for in the end he remains, by YHWH's word, YHWH's servant (42:8), just as in 1:8. YHWH's declaration about Job's speech should be determinative of the reader's opinion within the world of the book of Job. YHWH declares that, unlike the friends, Job has in the end spoken things of YHWH that can be considered "right," in the sense of "established," "sure" (HALOT, 464). This makes explicit what is implicit in the book's deafening omission. Nowhere, before, during, or after Job's speeches does YHWH indict Job in such a way as to expect Job to repent and pray for forgiveness and acceptance. Nowhere does YHWH list Job's sins in such a fashion as to validate Yhwh's action against Job in chapters 1 and 2.

Contrary to what one might think, however, this absence of divine indictment of Job is not because the topic of Job's possible sin has not entered the discussion beyond the accusations of his friends. We recall the assessment of Job's character from the introduction. By the narrator's assessment and by YHWH's word as well, Job was "perfect and upright, and one who feared God, and who turned from evil" (1:1 and 8). The writer extends this by telling us Job was so morally sensitive that he offered sacrifice for his children covering the possibility that they might have "cursed God in their hearts" (1:5).

In the parallel accounts in chapters 1 and 2 of Job's responses to the attacks of Satan on Job we note an intriguing development. At the conclusion of the first round of attacks on Job he offers a poetic assessment of the situation: "Blessed I came from my mother's womb // and naked I shall return there. YHWH has given, and YHWH has taken away. // Blessed be the name of YHWH." Then comes the narrator's assessment: "In all this Job did not sin, // nor did he cause offense to God" (1:21-22).

Then at the conclusion of the second round of assaults upon Job, after his wife's not so encouraging words—"Curse God and die!"—Job again offers a poetic response: "Will we receive good from God // and not also accept evil [from him]?" (2:10). Then the narrator offers this assessment. "In all this Job did not sin"—just as he had in 1:22. But then he continues: "…with his lips" (2:10). Job did not sin with his lips! Given the fact that the first half of a possible bicolon creates a space inviting the reader to finish it, and given the fact that the narrator has stressed the possibility of sinning "with the heart" and Job's own keen awareness of that sort of sin, we may not be surprised then when the Targum actually does finish the bicolon with the words, "But he did mutter words in his heart" (thoughts) ברם ברעיוניה הרהיר.

Just what is being implied in the MT is not entirely clear. Is it hinting that Job at his best was still not flawless? Was Eliphaz' claim actually true, that if God wished, he could find fault even with his angels (4:17-19)? If so, it simply adds to the book the insight that whatever fault God *could* have found in his servant Job, it was not, contrary to the insistence of the friends, a factor in Job's suffering. He was not suffering because of his sin, whether blatant and public or hidden in his heart. His moral deficiencies, if indeed he had any worth reckoning, were not related at all in this story to his suffering as the narrative runs. Indeed, if anything, Job suffered *because of* his righteousness, in so far as anything about Job led toward his pain.

And, YHWH did not mention anything about Job's muttering words in his heart, either in his speeches to Job or in his comments in the epilogue. And apparently the accusations YHWH does level against Job—that he spoke beyond his competence, and that he maligned God in the course of seeking to justify his responses to his friends and his strident remarks about and to God—apparently these two main accusations of YHWH against Job are not to be thought of as sins for which Job should repent or which disqualify him as one to whom YHWH can send the chastened friends for intercession on their behalf (42:8). All of this we bring to our reading of 42:1-6.

Job's Response to YHWH's Speeches

In our passage Job does five things. First, (42:2) he responds (*laken*) to the majority content of YHWH's interrogatory tour de force. YHWH said he would ask questions; this he has certainly done. Job's response is the claim, not necessarily a new insight, but certainly true, that "YHWH can do whatever he chooses. No one can thwart his plans." Repeatedly Job's speeches implied this—as did God's questions.

Second, he referenced God's accusation (38:2) that his repeated speech beyond competence (beyond his knowledge) had brought more confusion than clarity to the long and painful debate. This he admitted to be true. He had indeed spoken far beyond his competence (40:4; 42:3).

Third, and just as he had demanded in his misguided speeches, now Job says he has not only heard God but in this encounter with the whirlwind he has somehow "seen" God (42:5). Surely this should elevate the value of the words he is about to speak. Because of our focus we cannot pursue this, in spite of its import. Here Job knows his new "insights" have come from YHWH himself, from a revelation from beyond himself, from YHWH who has *allowed* himself to be seen.

Fourth, and as a response to the preceding, Job "recants" what he has said. Especially, I would think, he recants where he spoke far beyond his competence as a *geber*, as YHWH has rightly claimed. Here I am agreeing with those interpreters who make the syntactical observation that מאס takes a direct object, not a reflexive. The lexeme מאס in this instance therefore means Job "recanted" of an object we must supply (e.g., probably Job's words at certain points). He did not loath himself. If we have been correct to this point, Job has nothing for which to loathe himself beyond the situation in which YHWH has placed him.

Fifth he נחם / "*re*lents" concerning עפר ואפר. But what, to return to our first questions, do we make of his "relenting concerning dust and ashes?"

1. Did he repent of sin in dust and ashes? No. Neither the text nor the context really will allow this, in spite of the well-known translation tradition.

2. Did he repent of his finitude and frailty itself as though the עפר ואפר condition were itself a sin? Surely not. Our word pair, עפר ואפר is not sin, neither in Job nor anywhere else in the Bible.

3. Nor, did he recant and relent because he *was* עפר ואפר, not because this condition is sin, but simply because it is responsible for his predicament. Thus, "I recant and relent, *being but dust and ashes*" (TNK, italics added). Commenting on v. 6 TNK notes, "As translated, the second half [of the line] reflects Job's basic creature hood, the fact that unlike God, he is a mere mortal, *dust and ashes*. The preposition that opens this section is more naturally translated 'on,' however, and thus this phrase may be a prosaic notice that Job feels this way while he is mourning on a dust-heap." Perhaps, but I think there is much more to the story than simply the lamentable nature of the human condition. And, more seriously, if we go back to translating נחמתי על־עפר ואפר as though it located Job *on*

dust and ashes, we adopt as solution the rendering we thought to be impossible at the beginning.

4. Did Job repent or perhaps relent of being עפר ואפר with an attitude? Is his "confession" really a final act of defiance? "I'm sorry I'm human, God. But you can take this life and…." I doubt it for two reasons. First one must read against the grain of the story as we have it in order to get there. The epilogue does not treat Job as a defiant hero. Second, this sounds more twenty-first century "AD-ish" than Iron Age "BC-ish."

5. Did Job relent or change his mind regarding the appropriateness of remaining with עפר ואפר? Was he "foreswearing" the symbols of mourning (Habel, 1985:575-576)? Perhaps, especially if we had either one word or the other and not the whole expression עפר ואפר. It cannot be reduced to either of the nouns alone. We have instead an expression of abasement and dishonor more than mourning (chs 29-30). And one wonders whether such a final conclusion rises to the import of its place in the book.

6. Was Job simply disclosing that he was "comforted concerning the human condition?" (Perdue). Perhaps so. This is a possible translation. But one wonders if "comfort" is what one should expect as the result of the sort of confrontation with the Whirlwind that Job has just had and whether or not we should expect not simply comfort but also some sort of correction or redirection.

7. Perhaps, having retracted his previous words, Job has a reconception [i.e., "change of mind"] of the human condition in which, in Carol Newsom's words, "the vulnerability of the human existence can be understood, not in terms of divine enmity, but in terms of a creation within which the chaotic is restrained but never fully eliminated" (NIB, IV, 29). This rests on a suitable translation and makes progress I think, especially if one does not leave YHWH at the mercy of the chaotic. But I think further progress is possible.

8. I propose that Job retracts his incompetent pontifications and then confesses a profound change of mind regarding ואפר עפר, that is, regarding the human condition. For all its dignity and bestowed genius it yet remains essentially other than the Judge of All the Earth. It remains continually subject to the frailty and finitude that also mark humankind. Job's life-changing discovery in the hearing and seeing of YHWH was the discovery that human beings as עפר ואפר do not in themselves have sufficient knowledge or experience from which to understand what is happening to them, to unravel history—much less to explain the doings of the divine. We recall that none of the terra firma characters knew why Job was suffering, whether there was purpose in it or not. All of them were mistaken, their confidence notwithstanding.

We learn of the dignity and bestowed genius of human beings as עפר ואפר, especially in Abraham's standing with YHWH. This sounds like the life of Ps 8:4-5: "What is mankind / אֱנוֹשׁ that you are mindful of them, human beings that you care for them?" This was the sort of עפר ואפר Job experienced before the frightful days into which YHWH plunged him. This was the time of his chapter 29 years when his frailty and finitude were not so obvious. This was the time when one might actually be tempted to think עפר ואפר was indeed sufficiently competent that human beings, though "dust and ashes," could nevertheless go toe to toe with the Almighty.

Job's immersion in suffering and social upheaval threw all that into question. His new vision of Shaddai demolished that näivete. Only God can explain God, he learned, and God does not produce explanations on demand. Job became a critical realist regarding his existence as עפר ואפר. This reassessment of the עפר ואפר condition reminds one of the inter-textual pairing of Pss 8:5 with 9:20. There on the one hand in Ps 8, the psalmist marvels at the glory with which the Creator has crowned human beings (אֱנוֹשׁ /'enosh). "You have made him little less than God; you crown him with glory and honor." But then, in Ps 9:20, the psalmist asks YHWH to restrain 'enosh and to make human beings, who tend toward arrogance, to know they are just 'enosh. Sticking with the Psalter for a moment, it is Job's critical realism regarding עפר ואפר, that makes a way for the so-called songs of lament and their candid confrontation of YHWH.

Returning to Job and its place in the canon, Job asks implicitly for the Incarnation of the Son of God in order to respond adequately to questions raised by the book. Job also paves the way for the Incarnation with its critical realism regarding the human experience as עפר ואפר. Can there be incarnation if עפר ואפר is in itself a cause for repentance? Surely not, if the claims of 1 John 1:1-4 and 4:2 are true? On the other hand, can incarnation be adequately appreciated if the frailty and finitude of עפר ואפר is forgotten? I doubt it.

End Notes

[1] I am delighted to be included among those invited to submit writings in honor of Professor John Oswalt, himself a model of careful and edifying publication in the service of the church. He has lead the way in fearless writing for the academy, the Church and the world. Praise the Lord.

Works Cited

Curtis, John Briggs
    1979   "On Job's Response to Yahweh." *JBL* 98:497-511.

Habel, Norman C.
    1985   *The Book of Job: A Commentary*. Old Testament Library. Philadelphia, PA: The Westminster Press.

Hartley, John E.
    1988   *The Book of Job*. The New International Commentary on the Old Testament Grand Rapids, MI: William B. Eerdmans Publishing Company.

Kuyper, L, J.
    1959   "The Repentance of Job." *Vetus Testamentum*, 9(1): 91-94.

Newell, B.I.
    1984   "Job: Repentant or Rebellious." *WTJ* 46:298-316.

Newsom, Carol A.
    1996   "The Book of Job." Pages 319-637 of *The New Interpreter's Bible: Introduction, Commentary, and Reflections*. Nashville, TN: Abingdon Press.

Made in United States
Cleveland, OH
08 May 2025

16767754R00118